THE ULTIMATE HOCKEY TRIVIA CHALLENGE

OVER 600 QUIZ QUESTIONS
FOR DIE-HARD HOCKEY FANS

HANK PATTON

ISBN: 979-8-89095-056-7

Copyright © 2025 by Curious Press

ALL RIGHTS RESERVED

No part of this book may be reproduced, stored in a retrieval system, or transmitted in any form or by any means, electronic, mechanical, photocopying, recording, scanning, or otherwise, without the prior written permission of the publisher.

CONTENTS

Introduction 1

Chapter 1: Hockey's Beginnings and Development 3
    Chapter 1 Answers 8
    Did You Know? 9

Chapter 2: Amateur Hockey Association of Canada and Other Early Leagues 10
    Chapter 2 Answers 15
    Did You Know? 16

Chapter 3: More Early Leagues 17
    Chapter 3 Answers 22
    Did You Know? 23

Chapter 4: The National Hockey Association 24
    Chapter 4 Answers 29
    Did You Know? 30

Chapter 5: The National Hockey League is Born 31
    Chapter 5 Answers 36
    Did You Know? 37

Chapter 6: The 1920s 38
    Chapter 6 Answers 43
    Did You Know? 44

Chapter 7: The 1930s 45
    Chapter 7 Answers 50
    Did You Know? 51

Chapter 8: The 1940s 52
Chapter 8 Answers 57
Did You Know? 58

Chapter 9: The 1950s 59
Chapter 9 Answers 64
Did You Know? 65

Chapter 10: The 1960s 66
Chapter 10 Answers 71
Did You Know? 72

Chapter 11: The 1970s 73
Chapter 11 Answers 78
Did You Know? 79

Chapter 12: The 1980s 80
Chapter 12 Answers 85
Did You Know? 86

Chapter 13: The 1990s 87
Chapter 13 Answers 92
Did You Know? 93

Chapter 14: The 2000s 94
Chapter 14 Answers 99
Did You Know? 100

Chapter 15: The 2010s 101
Chapter 15 Answers 106
Did You Know? 107

Chapter 16: 2020-2024 108
Chapter 16 Answers 113
Did You Know? 114

Chapter 17: Mergers, Movers, and Growth 115

Chapter 17 Answers..119
Did You Know? 120

Chapter 18: The Western Conference... 121
Chapter 18 Answers..126
Did You Know? 127

Chapter 19: The Eastern Conference... 128
Chapter 19 Answers..133
Did You Know? 134

Chapter 20: The Metropolitan Division Part 1............................. 135
Chapter 20 Answers..139
Did You Know? 140

Chapter 21: The Metropolitan Division Part 2............................. 141
Chapter 21 Answers..146
Did You Know? 147

Chapter 22: The Atlantic Division Part 1 148
Chapter 22 Answers..153
Did You Know? 154

Chapter 23: The Atlantic Division Part 2 155
Chapter 23 Answers..160
Did You Know? 161

Chapter 24: The Central Division Part 1... 162
Chapter 24 Answers..167
Did You Know? 168

Chapter 25: The Central Division Part 2... 169
Chapter 25 Answers..174
Did You Know? 175

Chapter 26: The Pacific Division Part 1 176
Chapter 26 Answers..181

Did You Know? 182

Chapter 27: The Pacific Division Part 2 183
Chapter 27 Answers 188
Did You Know? 189

Chapter 28: MVP Seasons 190
Chapter 28 Answers 195
Did You Know? 196

Chapter 29: Stanley Cup Championships 197
Chapter 29 Answers 202
Did You Know? 203

Chapter 30: Hockey Hall of Fame 204
Chapter 30 Answers 209
Did You Know? 210

Chapter 31: Unbeatable Records 211
Chapter 31 Answers 216
Did You Know? 217

Chapter 32: The Biggest Moments 218
Chapter 32 Answers 223
Did You Know? 224

Chapter 33: The All-Star Game 225
Chapter 33 Answers 230
Did You Know? 231

Chapter 34: Hockey's Advanced Statistics 232
Chapter 34 Answers 234
Did You Know? 235

Conclusion 236

ATTENTION:

DO YOU WANT MY FUTURE BOOKS AT HEAVY DISCOUNTS AND EVEN FOR FREE?

HEAD OVER TO WWW.SECRETREADS.COM AND JOIN MY SECRET BOOK CLUB!

INTRODUCTION

Ice hockey is a sport with a very detailed history. The game has been entertaining fans around the world for almost 150 years, and although its popularity is not as extensive as other sports, it still attracts great athletes.

Hockey grew slowly but soon moved overseas. As the game has expanded over the years, rules have been adjusted to make it faster and to reward skill over strength. The first hockey organizations were formed in Canada, followed quickly by the United States and countries in Europe.

Today's hockey is the fastest it has ever been, and it features players who are more athletic and skilled than any group of players from the past. Though today's players are better, players from earlier years accomplished great things! This book will test how well you know these players, plus the sport's best moments and fun facts about it.

After all, the players of the past helped build the game up to what it is today. For instance, do you know who set the early records and helped teams win championships before the Stanley Cup progressed to its full size?

This book begins with the early history of the game, so those chapters might be very difficult but educational! Players, teams, and leagues left to history will be covered, testing even the best hockey students.

The best players from each team's history will also be featured, and many of today's stars will also make an appearance. There's plenty in this book for every hockey fan!

Do you have what it takes to answer the questions in each of these stimulating chapters? Can you overcome every challenge and prove your hockey knowledge dominance?

If not, don't worry! The answer sections will give the correct responses, along with a bit more information about almost every question. So, get your hockey family and friends together and enjoy these gritty questions!

The trivia puck drops now!

CHAPTER 1:
HOCKEY'S BEGINNINGS AND DEVELOPMENT

1. Which of these games from the Middle Ages is the most closely associated with the origins of ice hockey?

   A. Shinty
   B. Bandy
   C. Polo
   D. Skittles

2. Which of these Canadian First Nations peoples also played a similar stick and ball sport on ice during the early 1800s?

   A. Cree
   B. Abenaki
   C. Mi'kmaq
   D. Innu

3. An early form of hockey came from the Scottish game shinty, but what was it called?

   A. Shinny
   B. Lacrosse
   C. Bung
   D. Hurling

4. Because of a novel published in 1844 called *The Attache: Second Series*, historians believe hockey was invented in which of these Canadian provinces?

   A. Ontario
   B. Quebec
   C. New Brunswick
   D. Nova Scotia

5. The word "hockey" was used as far back as in which century in a book called *Juvenile Sports and Pastimes, to Which Are Prefixed, Memoirs of the Author: Including a New Mode of Infant Education*?

   A. 16th
   B. 17th
   C. 18th
   D. 19th

6. Which Canadian city is recognized as the birthplace of organized ice hockey?

    A. Quebec
    B. Montreal
    C. Halifax
    D. Ontario

7. The first organized ice hockey game played indoors featured how many players on each team?

    A. Five
    B. Nine
    C. 11
    D. 12

8. The first organized indoor game took place between two universities, James Creighton and which school?

    A. McGill University
    B. Dalhousie University
    C. Saint Mary's University
    D. University of New Brunswick

9. In 1876, as the game began to spread, games in Montreal were played using rules from which organization?

    A. McGill University Hockey Club
    B. Hockey Association
    C. Quebec Hockey Club
    D. Amateur Hockey Association of Canada

10. When *The Gazette* published a list of rules in the city of Montreal back in 1877, how many rules were included?

    A. Seven
    B. 10
    C. 12
    D. 15

11. Which of these hockey clubs was the first to be founded back in 1877?

    A. McGill University Hockey Club
    B. Quebec Hockey Club
    C. Montreal Victorias
    D. Oxford University Ice Hockey Club

12. As the game developed, the rules changed. In 1880, the number of players for each team decreased from nine to what number?

    A. Eight
    B. Seven
    C. Six
    D. Five

13. The first "world championship" in ice hockey was held during which event in Montreal?

    A. World Cup
    B. Winter Olympics
    C. Homecoming
    D. Winter Carnival

14. Of the six tournaments held from 1883 to 1889, which team won twice, including the final tournament in 1889?

    A. McGill University Ice Hockey Club
    B. Montreal Victorias
    C. Montreal Hockey Club
    D. Montreal Crystals

15. During the Winter Carnival tournaments, each game was played in which of these increments?

    A. Three periods of 20 minutes each
    B. Two halves of 20 minutes each
    C. Two halves of 30 minutes each
    D. Two halves of 45 minutes each

16. With seven players per side, what was the named position that represented the extra player compared to today's game?

    A. Rover
    B. Roamer
    C. Rounder
    D. Cover wing

17. The oldest rivalry in ice hockey history began in 1886 when Queen's University and Royal Military College played their first game. Which city were both of those schools from?

    A. Montreal
    B. Kingston

C. Halifax
D. Ottawa

18. In 1888, the Governor General of Canada attended the Montreal tournament for the first time. What was his title?

    A. The Marquess of Lansdowne
    B. The Earl of Aberdeen
    C. The Lord Stanley of Preston
    D. The Earl of Minto

Chapter 1 Answers:

1. B. Bandy. Though shinty and polo are also played with sticks curved at the end, bandy is the only sport played most typically on ice. This game formed in England in the 1800s before it was introduced to Canada by British soldiers.
2. C. Mi'kmaq. They called their game *tooadijik*, but the version they played on the ice was called *oochamkunutk*. One of their elders, Joe Cope, was famous for his carving talent, making what became some of the first hockey sticks ever used.
3. A. Shinny. The game is not played today, but the word "shinny" is now used to designate any informal game of hockey. While most sports would use the term "pick-up" to indicate the informality of the game, "shinny" has become its own noun to indicate an informal game of hockey.
4. D. Nova Scotia. Though there have been claims that the game was invented in Ontario, perhaps even at King's College School, there are other claims that the game was invented around the area of Dartmouth and Halifax, both of Nova Scotia.
5. C. 18th. The book mentioned was published in 1773, written by Richard Johnson. The 11th chapter of his book was titled "New Improvements on the Game of Hockey." A book published in 2014 called *On the Origin of Hockey* has more information if you're curious!
6. B. Montreal. This is because Montreal as a city played host to the first-ever organized indoor game of ice hockey back in 1875. However, that game did not resemble the modern game of ice hockey much at all.
7. B. Nine. That first game was played more like polo, with goal posts eight feet apart. They also used a piece of wood instead of a ball or "bung."
8. A. McGill University. McGill hosted the game, and many female fans left the game after seeing how violent and aggressive the players were behaving on the ice.
9. B. Hockey Association. It was the Hockey Association of England, which was in charge of England's field hockey rules.
10. A. Seven. Six of those rules were based on rules taken from the Hockey Association of England, and the only rule they added was

an explanation of how to handle disputes. It was a slow start, but it was the beginning of hockey growing into its own game.
11. A. McGill University Hockey Club. The Quebec Hockey Club was formed one year later, in 1878; then, the Montreal Victorias followed in 1881. There are reports that the Oxford University Ice Hockey Club formed in 1885, but there is no evidence of the team until 1895.
12. B. Seven. It was a step toward hockey looking more and more like the modern game, but there was still plenty that needed to change.
13. D. Winter Carnival. These tournaments are widely considered the first ice hockey championship competitions. After a few years, these tournaments led to the founding of the first championship ice hockey league.
14. B. Montreal Victorias. The McGill team only won the inaugural tournament in 1883. The Montreal Hockey Club also won twice, in 1885 and 1887. The Montreal Crystals only won in 1886 during the Dominion Championship, as the Winter Carnival was canceled that year.
15. C. Two halves of 30 minutes each. Though modern hockey would eventually split into three periods, it is interesting that this early iteration also had 60 minutes of playing time.
16. A. Rover. It was a position that would last for many more years before the game continued to evolve.
17. B. Kingston. The two teams play for the Carr-Harris Cup.
18. C. The Lord Stanley of Preston. That name might sound familiar to fans of the National Hockey League, and for good reason. He had a large role in helping hockey grow in Canada.

Did You Know?

Oxford University and Cambridge thought they had the oldest rivalry in hockey history, but their 1885 match was actually a game of bandy, not ice hockey.

CHAPTER 2:
AMATEUR HOCKEY ASSOCIATION OF CANADA AND OTHER EARLY LEAGUES

1. The Amateur Hockey Association of Canada (AHAC) was the first league to determine a champion, but it was not the first league in Canada. Where was the first league formed?

   A. Ontario
   B. Halifax
   C. Kingston
   D. Montreal

2. When the AHAC started play, the goals on each side of the ice only had what?

   A. Cross bars
   B. Netting
   C. Goal lines
   D. Goal posts

3. Though there were seven skaters on the ice for each team during league play in the AHAC, how many players were on each bench in reserve?

   A. Zero
   B. Three
   C. Seven
   D. Ten

4. Though the league eventually went to a series system that is similar to the modern NHL's regular season, what kind of system did they use for the first few years?

   A. Points
   B. Conference
   C. Challenge
   D. Promotion

5. Though the league's first season was in 1887, which year marked the first time the championship trophy from Lord Stanley of Preston was awarded?

   A. 1891
   B. 1892
   C. 1893
   D. 1894

6. The league had eight different teams compete, with only four to six teams playing per season. How many different teams won the championship?

   A. Three
   B. Four
   C. Five
   D. Six

7. The Senior Championship Trophy of the AHAC displayed how many player figurines on it?

   A. Two
   B. Three
   C. Four
   D. Five

8. The Manitoba Hockey Association held its first season in what year, one year after its founding?

   A. 1892
   B. 1893
   C. 1894
   D. 1895

9. The Manitoba Hockey Association existed for 12 seasons before it became a professional league in what year?

   A. 1900
   B. 1903
   C. 1905
   D. 1908

10. The Manitoba Professional Hockey League lasted for three years, and then when it folded, which nearby league took its place?

    A. Manitoba Hockey League
    B. Manitoba Hockey Players Association
    C. Manitoba Professional League
    D. Manitoba Hockey Association

11. Though the Manitoba Hockey Association expanded from two teams to five in 1904, the league only lasted for how many more years?

A. One
   B. Two
   C. Three
   D. Four

12. This league only lasted four seasons, but its move from amateur to professional led to the Stanley Cup only being contested by professional teams. Which league was this?

    A. Eastern Canada Amateur Hockey Association
    B. Western Pennsylvania Hockey League
    C. Canadian Amateur Hockey League
    D. Federal Amateur Hockey League

13. Owen McCourt died on the ice during a Federal Amateur Hockey League (FAHL) game while playing for which team?

    A. Montreal Le National
    B. Montreal Wanderers
    C. Cornwall Hockey Club
    D. Ottawa Capitals

14. Which FAHL team won the Stanley Cup in 1904 and 1905?

    A. Montreal Le National
    B. Montreal Wanderers
    C. Smiths Falls Hockey Club
    D. Ottawa Hockey Club

15. The final FAHL season in 1909 was won by which team?

    A. Cornwall
    B. Ottawa Senators
    C. Renfrew Creamery Kings
    D. Smiths Falls

16. The Western Pennsylvania Hockey League (WPHL) was formed in 1896, but it didn't finish its first season because of the impact of what on the main arena?

    A. Tornado
    B. Earthquake
    C. Fire
    D. Flood

17. The WPHL returned in 1899. Which of these teams won the league's first championship?
    A. Western University
    B. Duquesne C&AC
    C. Pittsburgh AC
    D. Keystones

18. The WPHL goes down in history as the first hockey league to do what?
    A. Play with only five skaters per side
    B. Openly hire professional players
    C. Play against the US National Team
    D. Last more than five years

Chapter 2 Answers:

1. C. Kingston. That league started four years before the AHAC, though it did not last very long.
2. D. Goal posts. The goals did not have nets or cross bars. In fact, players playing the goalie position did not have any special equipment. It was likely a dangerous assignment.
3. A. Zero. Each player on the ice had to play all 60 minutes with no substitutions, but they did get a ten-minute intermission break between halves. There were also rules about players being replaced in the case of an injury during play, but there is little evidence that many teams had more than one or two players on standby.
4. C. Challenge. This meant that one team would be the championship team, and they would have to play against a new challenger each week. If they lost, they were replaced. The team at the top when the season ended was the champion.
5. C. 1893. It was the second year that the league used the series system, and the trophy was won by Montreal HC. The league would not return to the challenge system despite the travel costs for many teams in the league.
6. A. Three. Montreal HC won the championship seven years in a row. The Montreal Crystals won the first championship in 1887, and the Montreal Victorias won the final four championships of the league's existence.
7. A. Two. Though the trophy had two player figures, one on each side of the trophy, both of those player figurines have been lost to time. The trophy exists today with neither figurine.
8. B. 1893. The league began as an amateur league for elite players, but it would eventually make the jump to a professional league. Yes, there were multiple professional leagues competing back in the early days!
9. C. 1905. The league had absorbed the Manitoba & Northwestern Hockey Association league the year before, and that included the addition of the Rat Portage/Kenora Thistles team from Ontario.
10. A. Manitoba Hockey League. The league was considered one of the best, but teams in Western Canada were not yet allowed to challenge for the national championship at the time.

11. B. Two. The Rat Portage Thistles and Kenora Thistles won the final two championships before the league folded.
12. A. Eastern Canada Amateur Hockey Association. The league formed in 1905, taking teams from the Canadian Amateur Hockey League and the FAHL.
13. C. Cornwall Hockey Club. The 1906–07 season ended early because of the incident, and Charles Masson of the Ottawa Victorias was found not guilty of manslaughter for McCourt's death.
14. D. Ottawa Hockey Club. They also had the best record in the FAHL during the 1904–05 season. They were the only FAHL team during the FAHL's existence to win the Stanley Cup.
15. C. Renfrew Creamery Kings. It was the team's first year in existence, and they would go on to play in the National Hockey Association for two more seasons before folding.
16. C. Fire. The Schenley Park Casino was the first arena in North America to produce an artificial ice surface. An ammonia pipe leaked and caused an explosion and fire on December 17, 1896.
17. C. Pittsburgh AC. They would win the first three championships in the league, but they would not win again after that opening streak.
18. B. Openly hire professional players. Other leagues were amateur in status, and some of those would pay players in secret to attract talent. There are also inklings that the WPHL was the first league to be involved in a trade between players, but the evidence is shaky.

Did You Know?

The Stanley Cup was donated in 1892 but wasn't used as the championship trophy of the NHL until 1926.

CHAPTER 3:
MORE EARLY LEAGUES

1. The International Professional Hockey League (IPHL) was founded in which year?

    A. 1904
    B. 1905
    C. 1906
    D. 1907

2. The IPHL was founded by Jack "Doc" Gibson, but what kind of doctor was he?

    A. Surgeon
    B. Pediatrician
    C. Dentist
    D. Optometrist

3. Two cities in the IPHL had the same name. Which of these was it?

    A. Pittsburgh
    B. Calumet
    C. Houghton
    D. Sault Ste. Marie

4. The first championship in the IPHL went to Calumet-Laurium. What was their team's name?

    A. Indians
    B. Soo
    C. Miners
    D. Flyers

5. The Timiskaming Professional Hockey League (TPHL) tried to compete for the Stanley Cup twice in 1909, but why were they rejected?

    A. Gambling allegations
    B. Paying ringers
    C. Bribing referees
    D. Only having two teams

6. Which was the last team to win the TPHL championship in 1911?

    A. Cobalt Silver Kings
    B. Haileybury Comets
    C. New Liskeard, Ontario
    D. North Bay, Ontario

7. Ambrose O'Brien owned two teams in the TPHL, and his family's success allowed him to fund how many teams for the newly formed National Hockey Association (NHA)?

   A. Two
   B. Three
   C. Four
   D. Five

8. When the TPHL folded before the 1910 season, how many of its teams helped form the NHA?

   A. One
   B. Two
   C. Three
   D. Four

9. The Ontario Professional Hockey League (OPHL) was founded in 1907, and in their first season, which team challenged for the Stanley Cup but lost?

   A. Berlin Dutchmen
   B. Brantford Indians
   C. Guelph Royals
   D. Toronto Pros

10. Which team initially showed interest in joining the OPHL but skipped the first season?

    A. Berlin Dutchmen
    B. Galt Professionals
    C. St. Catharines Pros
    D. Guelph Royals

11. Which league raided the NHA for players, just as the NHA had raided the OPHL for players in 1911, after the OPHL folded?

    A. Pacific Coast Hockey Association
    B. Western Pennsylvania Hockey League
    C. Maritime Professional Hockey League
    D. Eastern Canada Amateur Hockey Association

12. Which two brothers were instrumental in starting the Pacific Coast Hockey Association (PCHA) and had a big impact on hockey history?

A. Patrick brothers
   B. Ross brothers
   C. Stanley brothers
   D. Richard brothers

13. When the PCHA began with three teams, how many players were under contract?

    A. 22
    B. 23
    C. 24
    D. 25

14. The first PCHA champions, winners of the Patterson Cup, were which team?

    A. Vancouver Millionaires
    B. Victoria Senators
    C. New Westminster Royals
    D. Portland Rosebuds

15. Cyclone Taylor signed a contract with the Vancouver Millionaires in 1912 for how much money, the most of any player at the time?

    A. $1,000/year
    B. $1,400/year
    C. $1,800/year
    D. $2,000/year

16. In 1914–1915, the Vancouver Millionaires defeated which NHA team, becoming the first PCHA team to win the Stanley Cup?

    A. Montreal Canadiens
    B. Toronto Hockey Club
    C. Ottawa Senators
    D. Toronto St. Patricks

17. In 1911, the PCHA introduced what to their league, the first time it had been used in either of the major hockey leagues?

    A. Player numbers
    B. Playoffs
    C. Line changes
    D. Major penalties

18. After being the first American team to ever win the Stanley Cup just four years earlier, which PCHA team folded in 1924?

   A. Portland Rosebuds
   B. Seattle Metropolitans
   C. Regina Capitals
   D. Chicago Black Hawks

Chapter 3 Answers:

1. A. 1904. The league would play until it was stopped in 1907, and it had a big role in bringing professional hockey into a more popular standing.
2. C. Dentist. Perhaps Gibson saw ice hockey as a good investment for a dental business!
3. D. Sault Ste. Marie. Neither of those teams would win a championship in the league, even though they made up 40% of the teams in the league.
4. C. Miners. The other two league championships would go to the Houghton-Portage Lakes team.
5. B. Paying ringers. Many big players from the early NHL were suspected as ringers in the TPHL, including Art Ross, Harry Smith, and Newsy Lalonde.
6. A. Cobalt Silver Kings. They were the team rejected by the Stanley Cup trustees for allegedly paying ringers to help them in single games.
7. C. Four. One of those teams was known as "Les Canadiens," who are now known as the Montreal Canadiens. Without the TPHL, one of the NHL's Original Six might never have existed.
8. B. Two. The Cobalt Silver Kings and the Haileybury Comets, both owned by Ambrose O'Brien, were the teams that helped form the NHA.
9. D. Toronto Pros. They lost to the Montreal Wanderers of the ECAHA.
10. B. Galt Professionals. They won the league championship when they joined the league in its second season. They also won the last league championship in 1911.
11. A. Pacific Coast Hockey Association. It was a league that operated from 1912 to 1924.
12. A. Patrick brothers. Lester and Frank, using money from their father's lumber company, founded the league and had a big impact on hockey history along the way.
13. B. 23. Every player in the league was paid by the league, not the individual teams. There were also two reserve players shared by every team in case of injury.

14. C. New Westminster Royals. They only had to defeat two other teams and achieve the best record, but it was the start of a league that was poised to make big changes to the game of hockey.
15. C. $1,800/year. Taylor had even turned down a contract with the Ottawa Hockey Club of the NHA to play in the PCHA.
16. C. Ottawa Senators. It was also the first Stanley Cup awarded after the end of the Challenge Cup era.
17. A. Player numbers. It was the first time numbers were used to identify players on the ice for the purposes of refereeing.
18. B. Seattle Metropolitans. They won the Stanley Cup in 1917, defeating the Montreal Canadiens 3-1 to win the title.

Did You Know?

Hockey pucks are kept frozen before games to keep them from bouncing too much on the ice.

CHAPTER 4:
THE NATIONAL HOCKEY ASSOCIATION

1. When the National Hockey Association (NHA) began play in 1910, they immediately suspended the season to absorb how many teams from the Canadian Hockey Association?

    A. One
    B. Two
    C. Three
    D. Four

2. In which season did the NHA drop the rover position, bringing each team to six skaters on the ice at one time?

    A. 1911–12
    B. 1912–13
    C. 1913–14
    D. 1914–15

3. For the 1912–13 season, the NHA expanded to how many teams?

    A. Five
    B. Six
    C. Seven
    D. Eight

4. Which team repeated as league champions in 1912–13, even though many of their players had left for the PCHA?

    A. Montreal Canadiens
    B. Montreal Wanderers
    C. Ottawa Senators
    D. Quebec Bulldogs

5. After the 1912–13 season, the NHA and PCHA reached an agreement to stop poaching each other's players. How many years was the agreement?

    A. Three
    B. Four
    C. Five
    D. Six

6. In the 1910 NHA season, which player was the leading scorer, with 38 goals?

    A. Didier Pitre
    B. Joe Hall

    C. Newsy Lalonde
    D. Cyclone Taylor

7. Which of these changes to hockey was not made by the NHA?

    A. On-the-fly line changes
    B. Match penalties
    C. Splitting the game into three periods
    D. Forward passing

8. The NHA's O'Brien Cup was made of what material?

    A. Silver
    B. Gold
    C. Platinum
    D. Bronze

9. How many NHL teams from the modern day have their roots connected to the NHA days?

    A. One
    B. Two
    C. Three
    D. Four

10. During the 1910 season in the NHA, which team finished in last place?

    A. Montreal Shamrocks
    B. Les Canadiens
    C. Haileybury Hockey Club
    D. Cobalt Silver Kings

11. Three teams finished the 1910 NHA season with winning records, but which team only lost one of their 12 games?

    A. Montreal Wanderers
    B. Ottawa Hockey Club
    C. Renfrew Creamery Kings
    D. Cobalt Silver Kings

12. When NHA president Frank Robinson submitted a letter of resignation in October 1917, it was ignored, and he was voted to another term. Who took care of the league when Robinson did not return?

A. George Kennedy
   B. Eddie Livingstone
   C. Lester Patrick
   D. Frank Calder

13. Marty Walsh led the NHA in scoring during the 1910–11 season while playing for which team, the winners of the league championship?

   A. Montreal Canadiens
   B. Ottawa Hockey Club
   C. Quebec Bulldogs
   D. Montreal Wanderers

14. During the 1910–11 season in the NHA, what was the salary cap per team?

   A. $4,000
   B. $4,800
   C. $5,000
   D. $6,000

15. In the 1911–12 NHA season, which of these teams won the league championship and the Stanley Cup?

   A. Ottawa Hockey Club
   B. Quebec Bulldogs
   C. Montreal Wanderers
   D. Montreal Canadiens

16. On March 16, 1912, the NHA held an All-Star game for which player, who was injured in a car accident?

   A. Clint Benedict
   B. Harry Broadbent
   C. Eddie Gerard
   D. Bruce Ridpath

17. Which player was charged with assault at the beginning of the 1912–13 season when a brawl broke out between the Canadiens and Wanderers?

   A. Sprague Cleghorn
   B. Joe Malone

C. Rusty Crawford
D. Ken Randall

18. During the 1913–14 season, referees started doing what for the first time?

    A. Calling delayed penalties
    B. Dropping the puck for faceoffs
    C. Blowing the whistle for offsides
    D. Using hand motions to indicate penalty calls

Chapter 4 Answers:

1. B. Two. The Ottawa Hockey Club and Montreal Shamrocks both joined the league, which resumed play just ten days later.
2. A. 1911–12. Other leagues would not make this change until the 1920s, and other attempts to bring the rover position back would ultimately prove unsuccessful.
3. B. Six. Two new teams joined, and they were both from Toronto. One would later be called the "Blueshirts," and the other was called the "Tecumsehs."
4. D. Quebec Bulldogs. It would be the last championship that the team would ever win, though.
5. B. Four. The two leagues also set up an interleague draft, and they agreed to respect each other's reserve clauses. It was the first time the "option" to re-sign was added to hockey contracts.
6. C. Newsy Lalonde. Lalonde played professionally until 1927 when he retired. In 1950, he was inducted into the Hockey Hall of Fame for his great scoring ability.
7. D. Forward passing. The ability to pass the puck forward was not allowed until the NHL came around. Even then, they needed more time to allow forward passing in the offensive zone.
8. A. Silver. It was the championship trophy awarded to winners in the NHA and NHL until 1926, when there were no professional teams outside of the NHL left to compete for the Stanley Cup.
9. C. Three. The Montreal Canadiens, Toronto Maple Leafs, and Ottawa Senators all have connections to the NHA, though the Leafs do not claim the history of the Toronto Blueshirts. The Senators also have a gap when the franchise left and rebuilt.
10. B. Les Canadiens. They won two of their 12 games that season, scoring 59 goals and allowing 100 goals against. On average, they lost each game 8–5.
11. A. Montreal Wanderers. In their 12 games, they scored 91 goals and only allowed 41 goals. It was a dominant performance for the small league.
12. D. Frank Calder. Calder would need that experience, too, because he would go on to help the NHA transfer into the NHL, and he would serve as the first president of the NHL.

13. B. Ottawa Hockey Club. Ottawa won 13 of their 16 games, and Marty Walsh scored 35 of their 122 goals.
14. C. $5,000. Players were not happy with this amount, and while there were talks of players' unions forming, they never did.
15. B. Quebec Bulldogs. They won ten of their 18 games, but they scored the second-fewest goals during the season. The Canadiens, in last place of the four teams, won eight of their 18 games.
16. D. Bruce Ridpath. He never played hockey again, but he served as the manager for the Toronto Blueshirts for one year before resigning. He wanted to play, but both his hearing and vision had been too damaged from the accident.
17. A. Sprague Cleghorn. Even worse, the game was a pre-season exhibition. The brawl took place during a game that did not count in the standings.
18. B. Dropping the puck for faceoffs. Before this season, referees would place the puck on the ice. How their hands survived is a mystery!

Did You Know?

Women's ice hockey was not an Olympic event until 1998, some 70+ years after men's ice hockey.

CHAPTER 5:
THE NATIONAL HOCKEY LEAGUE IS BORN

1. The NHA's playing schedule was affected when which team withdrew from play during the 1916–1917 season?

    A. Toronto Hockey Club
    B. Toronto 228th Battalion
    C. Quebec Bulldogs
    D. Montreal Wanderers

2. To solve the NHA's scheduling problem, the other team owners voted to also remove which team, leaving four teams to compete in the second half of the season?

    A. Toronto Hockey Club
    B. Ottawa Senators
    C. Quebec Bulldogs
    D. Montreal Wanderers

3. Though the NHL played its first season in 1917, there were no teams from the United States until what year?

    A. 1921
    B. 1924
    C. 1926
    D. 1930

4. The NHL continued to face teams from other hockey leagues for the Stanley Cup, with the Cup being awarded as an inter-league trophy for the last time in what year?

    A. 1925
    B. 1926
    C. 1927
    D. 1928

5. A fire in which team's arena caused them to cease team operations permanently in 1918?

    A. Quebec Bulldogs
    B. Toronto Blueshirts
    C. Vancouver Millionaires
    D. Montreal Wanderers

6. Which team would go on to defeat the Vancouver Millionaires for the 1918 Stanley Cup and was the first team to win an NHL title?

A. Toronto Hockey Club
   B. Montreal Canadiens
   C. Ottawa Senators
   D. Detroit Cougars

7. Which player scored 44 goals in the first 20 games of the NHL's existence, even scoring five on opening night?

   A. Dave Ritchie
   B. Cy Denneny
   C. Bert Lindsay
   D. Joe Malone

8. The 1919 Stanley Cup series was not finished because of a flu epidemic. How many games did they play before canceling it?

   A. Two
   B. Three
   C. Four
   D. Five

9. For the 1918–19 season, a new rule stated that a minor penalty would result in a player sitting for how many minutes?

   A. Two
   B. Three
   C. Four
   D. One

10. The 1918–1919 season also saw the league's first use of what, adding more separation?

    A. Periods
    B. Blue lines
    C. Timeouts
    D. Penalty shots

11. The 1918–19 season would be the last for which team, as their financial difficulties could not be overcome?

    A. Ottawa Senators
    B. Montreal Canadiens
    C. Toronto Arenas
    D. Toronto St. Patricks

12. Which player led the league in scoring during the 1919–20 season, even though his team did not perform well?

    A. Joe Malone
    B. Hap Holmes
    C. Punch Broadbent
    D. Clint Benedict

13. The end of World War I brought many fans back to the seats in 1920. What was the record crowd on February 21, 1920?

    A. 6,500
    B. 7,500
    C. 8,500
    D. 9,500

14. Clint Benedict was the only goaltender to earn any shutouts during the 1919–20 season. How many shutouts did he collect that year?

    A. Three
    B. Five
    C. Six
    D. One

15. The record for most goals by one team in one game was set by the Canadiens during the 1919–20 season. How many goals did they score?

    A. 14
    B. 15
    C. 16
    D. 17

16. Babe Dye made his NHL debut with the Toronto St. Patricks during the 1919–20 season. What year was he inducted into the Hockey Hall of Fame?

    A. 1966
    B. 1967
    C. 1969
    D. 1970

17. The 1920 Stanley Cup Finals had to be moved away from Ottawa because of poor ice conditions. Where did they play Ottawa's home games for the rest of the series?

    A. Montreal
    B. Winnipeg
    C. Toronto
    D. Calgary

18. How much money did each Ottawa Senators player receive as a prize for playing in the 1920 Stanley Cup Finals?

    A. $250.00
    B. $287.63
    C. $390.19
    D. $411.64

Chapter 5 Answers:

1. B. Toronto 228th Battalion. In February 1917, the team was ordered overseas to fight in World War I.
2. A. Toronto Hockey Club. This decision sparked a lot of protest, which led to the demise of the NHA. It made room for the NHL to take its place one year later.
3. B. 1924. The Boston Bruins joined the league that year, though there were many more teams to follow in the next two years.
4. B. 1926. The Canadiens defeated the Victoria Cougars of the WHL. When the WHL folded, many of the players from the Cougars went to Detroit, where a new expansion team was forming in the NHL.
5. D. Montreal Wanderers. They were replaced by the Montreal Maroons, and though the new owners tried to use the Wanderers' name, they could not get the rights.
6. A. Toronto Hockey Club. After the NHL began, only one team not in the NHL won the Stanley Cup. The Victoria Cougars beat the Canadiens in 1925.
7. D. Joe Malone. His scoring attracted fans to the league. Dave Ritchie scored the first goal in league history, though.
8. D. Five. Several players got sick during the series. Joe Hall of the Montreal Canadiens died four days after contracting the illness, and their manager, George Kennedy, was left weakened for the rest of his life, dying two years later.
9. B. Three. Don't worry, though. That player's team was allowed to put a substitute player on the ice, meaning that there was no power play or penalty kill for minor penalties.
10. B. Blue lines. The middle neutral zone that was created by these lines did allow for forward passing and kicking of the puck, but not in the attacking zone.
11. C. Toronto Arenas. It didn't help that they finished in last place in both halves of the regular season that year. Toronto would reorganize and return the following season as the St. Patricks.
12. A. Joe Malone. He scored seven goals in one game for the Quebec Athletics and scored six on another occasion against the eventual champion, the Ottawa Senators. His 39 goals were the most in the league that year.

13. C. 8,500. They packed the Arena Gardens to see their Toronto St. Patricks play against the Ottawa Senators.
14. B. Five. His goals-against average (GAA) was 2.66, the best in the league. The next closest goalie had a GAA of 4.20, showing how big the gap was between Benedict, his Senators, and the rest of the league that season.
15. C. 16. They beat the Quebec Athletics 16–3. Things would have to change quite dramatically in today's game if this record is ever going to be beaten!
16. D. 1970. Dye played 11 seasons in the NHL, and he is remembered for his stick-handling skill as well as his goal-scoring abilities. He died eight years before his induction into the Hall.
17. C. Toronto. They played Game 3 in Ottawa but made the move to Toronto for Game 4, despite protests from the Ottawa team.
18. C. $390.19. In contrast, each player from the Seattle Metropolitans received $319.39. It was only a $70 difference between winning and losing the series, which Ottawa won in five games, 3–2.

Did You Know?

The "Zamboni" was named after Frank Zamboni, who invented the ice resurfacing machine in 1949.

CHAPTER 6:
THE 1920S

1. The Quebec franchise moved to which city for the 1920–21 season?
   A. Hamilton, Ontario
   B. Winnipeg, Manitoba
   C. Calgary, Alberta
   D. Vancouver, British Colombia

2. The 1920–21 season would be the last to use a split-season format. Which team won the second half of the season to compete for the O'Brien Cup?
   A. Ottawa Senators
   B. Toronto St. Patricks
   C. Hamilton Tigers
   D. Montreal Canadiens

3. During the 1921–22 season, another league was competing with the NHL and PCHA for the Stanley Cup. Which league was it?
   A. International Professional Hockey League
   B. Western Pennsylvania Hockey League
   C. Manitoba Professional Hockey League
   D. Western Canada Hockey League

4. The 1921–22 season changed a minor penalty to what number of minutes in the penalty box?
   A. One
   B. Two
   C. Three
   D. Four

5. On February 14, 1923, CFCA, a radio station of which newspaper was the first to ever broadcast an NHL game over the radio?
   A. The Gazette
   B. Le Presse
   C. The Toronto Daily Star
   D. The National Post

6. Cy Denneny passed Joe Malone during the 1922–23 season as the league's all-time leading scorer. How many goals did Denneny score?
   A. 143
   B. 151

    C. 170
    D. 173

7. The 1923–24 season was the first time that which trophy was awarded at the end of the year?

    A. Vezina Trophy
    B. Art Ross Trophy
    C. Hart Trophy
    D. Presidents' Trophy

8. Which team won the NHL championship in 1924, upsetting the Ottawa Senators, who had finished ahead of them in the standings by three games?

    A. Toronto St. Patricks
    B. Hamilton Tigers
    C. Seattle Metropolitans
    D. Montreal Canadiens

9. Which team finished with the best record during the 1924–25 regular season but refused to play in the playoffs because they demanded more pay?

    A. Montreal Canadiens
    B. Toronto St. Patricks
    C. Hamilton Tigers
    D. Ottawa Senators

10. With two new teams joining the league for the 1924–25 season, which team finished in last place out of the six competing teams?

    A. Ottawa Senators
    B. Boston Bruins
    C. Montreal Maroons
    D. Toronto St. Patricks

11. Which device, used to indicate the end of a period by the timekeeper, was first implemented as a rule during the 1925–26 NHL season?

    A. Horn
    B. Gong
    C. Bell
    D. Whistle

12. On December 15, 1925, the NHL played its first game in Madison Square Garden. The winning team of that game was awarded what new trophy for the first time?

    A. King Clancy Trophy
    B. Selke Trophy
    C. Prince of Wales Trophy
    D. Vezina Trophy

13. Which new team won their division in the 1926-27 season, though they did not win the Stanley Cup?

    A. Detroit Cougars
    B. Ottawa Senators
    C. New York Rangers
    D. Boston Bruins

14. The Detroit Cougars had to play their first 22 home games in which city because their home arena was not yet finished?

    A. Ann Arbor
    B. Chicago
    C. Ontario
    D. Lansing

15. Which Montreal Canadiens player won both the season MVP and top scorer awards at the end of the 1927-28 season?

    A. Howie Morenz
    B. Punch Broadbent
    C. Eddie Shore
    D. Frank Boucher

16. Which goalie won his second straight Vezina Trophy in 1927-28, awarded to the goaltender who allowed the fewest goals during the season?

    A. Tiny Thompson
    B. George Hainsworth
    C. Roy Worters
    D. Charlie Gardiner

17. In the final game of the regular season, what did the league allow to be legal for the first time?

    A. Two-line passes
    B. Penalty shots
    C. Handpasses
    D. Forward passes in the offensive zone
18. Which Bruins player was the first NHL player to wear protective headgear regularly?
    A. George Owen
    B. Harry Oliver
    C. Myles Lane
    D. Bill Carson

Chapter 6 Answers:

1. A. Hamilton, Ontario. They became the Hamilton Tigers, a team that would play in the NHL until 1925.
2. B. Toronto St. Patricks. They finished second in the first half of the season but could not overcome the Ottawa Senators in the championship series.
3. D. Western Canada Hockey League. The WCHL and PCHA had to play each other for a chance to play against the NHL champions.
4. B. Two. It also marked the first time that minor penalties led to penalty kills for the offending team. Penalized players were no longer allowed to be substituted on the ice.
5. C. *The Toronto Daily Star*. But they only had the broadcast running for the third period of the game between the Senators and the St. Patricks.
6. A. 143. Denneny scored a goal during Ottawa's 2-0 shutout of the Montreal Canadiens. Even better, the Senators went on to win both the NHL championship and the Stanley Cup.
7. C. Hart Trophy. It was the first time that the MVP of the league was awarded at the end of the year. The first award did not go to the top scorer of the league, either.
8. D. Montreal Canadiens. They defeated Ottawa 5-2 on total goals, then went on to defeat the Vancouver Maroons and the Calgary Tigers to claim the Stanley Cup.
9. C. Hamilton Tigers. They wanted $200 more per player for the six extra games. The league declined that offer, and the team decided to eliminate themselves from the playoffs.
10. B. Boston Bruins. They only won six games out of 30, scoring 49 goals and allowing 119 goals against.
11. B. Gong. This was used instead of the referee keeping track of the time and blowing the whistle to end a period.
12. C. Prince of Wales Trophy. After being awarded to the Canadiens for winning that game, it would be awarded to the team that won the NHL playoffs until the Stanley Cup took that spot.
13. C. New York Rangers. They finished four games ahead of the Boston Bruins, but they lost to the Bruins in the semifinals of the playoffs.

14. C. Ontario. They had to play in the Border Cities Arena while they waited for Olympia Stadium to finish construction.
15. A. Howie Morenz. He finished the season with 33 goals and 18 assists. With 51 points, he had 12 more points than the next closest player, his teammate, Aurel Joliat.
16. B. George Hainsworth. He would win the first three Vezina Trophies while playing with the Montreal Canadiens.
17. D. Forward passes in the offensive zone. The league wanted to increase scoring, so they experimented with the final game of the regular season and liked the results.
18. A. George Owen. Before Owen, protective helmets were only used to temporarily protect players who had suffered injuries. The NHL would not mandate helmets for another 51 years.

Did You Know?

The 1992–93 Pittsburgh Penguins hold the league record for longest winning streak at 17 games.

CHAPTER 7:
THE 1930S

1. For the 1930–31 season, the Detroit Cougars changed their team name to what?

    A. Red Wings
    B. Falcons
    C. Lions
    D. Tigers

2. Which team won a double-overtime game and a triple-overtime game in the 1931 Stanley Cup Finals but still lost to the Montreal Canadiens?

    A. Detroit Falcons
    B. New York Rangers
    C. Boston Bruins
    D. Chicago Black Hawks

3. During the 1931–32 season, Howie Morenz won another MVP award, but which player led the league in scoring?

    A. Busher Jackson
    B. Joe Primeau
    C. Charlie Conacher
    D. Bill Cook

4. Which goaltender had an impressive 1.85 GAA, leading the NHL during the 1931–32 season?

    A. Alec Connell
    B. George Hainsworth
    C. Charlie Gardiner
    D. John Ross Roach

5. The Boston Bruins tied with which team for the NHL's best record during the 1932–33 season?

    A. New York Rangers
    B. Toronto Maple Leafs
    C. Montreal Maroons
    D. Detroit Red Wings

6. The first forfeit in NHL history happened during the 1932–33 season when which team's coach got into a fistfight with the referee over a disputed goal?

A. Chicago Black Hawks
   B. New York Rangers
   C. Montreal Maroons
   D. New York Americans

7. After the Toronto Maple Leafs, which team became the second in league history to use a second set of jerseys, which they introduced during the 1933–34 NHL season?

   A. Chicago Black Hawks
   B. New York Rangers
   C. Montreal Maroons
   D. New York Americans

8. Which team had the best regular season record, with Charlie Conacher leading the scoring, but couldn't win in the playoffs?

   A. Chicago Black Hawks
   B. Detroit Red Wings
   C. Toronto Maple Leafs
   D. Montreal Maroons

9. The penalty shot was introduced during the 1934–35 season, but the player had to shoot from a circle that was how far away from the goal?

   A. 38 feet
   B. 35 feet
   C. 40 feet
   D. 24 feet

10. Which of these NHL teams moved away because of financial difficulties, becoming the St. Louis Eagles in the 1934–35 season?

    A. Chicago Black Hawks
    B. Ottawa Senators
    C. Montreal Maroons
    D. New York Americans

11. Which Bruins player was named MVP for the 1935–36 season, even though the Bruins did not make it past the first round of the playoffs?

    A. Eddie Shore
    B. Red Beattie

C. Cooney Weiland
   D. Percy Jackson

12. The Detroit Red Wings needed how many overtime periods to beat the Montreal Maroons in the first game of their semifinal series?

    A. Three
    B. Four
    C. Five
    D. Six

13. Who had been naming the year's best rookies since the 1932-33 season and bought a trophy to award to the best rookie each year beginning with the 1936-37 season?

    A. Georges Vezina
    B. Art Ross
    C. Frank Calder
    D. Carl Voss

14. Normie Smith of which team won the Vezina Trophy during the 1936-37 season, helping his team to win the Stanley Cup?

    A. Chicago Black Hawks
    B. New York Rangers
    C. Montreal Maroons
    D. Detroit Red Wings

15. Beginning with the 1937-38 season, which infraction was enforced?

    A. Offsides
    B. Two-line pass
    C. Icing
    D. Handpass

16. Neil Colville of which team was sidelined when a defenseman of his team, Joe Cooper, was trying to play a prank on him by cutting his necktie with a penknife and got Colville's hand instead?

    A. Chicago Black Hawks
    B. New York Rangers
    C. Montreal Canadiens
    D. New York Americans

17. The 1938–39 season marked the first time for what in the Stanley Cup Finals?

    A. A seven-game series
    B. Golden goal overtime
    C. A 2-2-1 schedule
    D. Skating with the trophy

18. The NHL's first game to be broadcast on TV was on February 25, 1940. How many people saw the small regional broadcast?

    A. 200
    B. 300
    C. 400
    D. 500

Chapter 7 Answers:

1. B. Falcons. The Detroit Falcons only lasted until 1932 before the switch was made to the team's current name, the Red Wings.
2. D. Chicago Black Hawks. They won Games 2 and 3 in double and triple overtime, but the Canadiens came back to win the series 3-2.
3. A. Busher Jackson. He collected 53 points in 48 games to help the Maple Leafs win the Stanley Cup.
4. C. Charlie Gardiner. Despite leading the league in that category, he finished the season with a losing record of 18 wins, 19 losses, and 11 ties.
5. D. Detroit Red Wings. The Bruins were awarded the division crown, as they had a better head-to-head record against Detroit.
6. A. Chicago Blackhawks. Ironically, that referee, Bill Stewart, would end up becoming Chicago's coach seasons later, and he would lead the team to a Stanley Cup.
7. D. New York Americans. Their home uniform had the word "Americans" across the front, while their away uniform had a shield logo on the front.
8. C. Toronto Maple Leafs. Conacher and the Leafs lost the five-game series against the Red Wings by a count of 3-2.
9. A. 38 feet. The circle was ten feet in diameter, and the player could choose to move around in it, but they had to shoot from the circle. Goalies had to stay still until the shot was taken, and they were only allowed to be one foot in front of the goal line.
10. B. Ottawa Senators. The new team did not perform well, only winning 11 of their 48 games in the season, finishing dead last.
11. A. Eddie Shore. Shore was the team's captain, but he did not lead the squad in any of the tracked statistical categories during the season.
12. D. Six. The Red Wings won the game by a score of 1-0, then won the series 3-0. They would go on to win the Stanley Cup to finish the season.
13. C. Frank Calder. Syl Apps was the first recipient of the new trophy, and the Calder Trophy still goes to the league's best rookie every year.
14. D. Detroit Red Wings. Smith had a GAA of 2.05 and six shutouts. He played every minute of the season for the team.

15. C. Icing. The league saw that teams were shooting the puck the length of the ice to waste time, so they wanted to cut that out of the game.
16. B. New York Rangers. Coach Lester Patrick was likely not happy when Colville needed 11 stitches to close the gash in his hand.
17. A. A seven-game series. The previous Finals had been five-game series; the increased number of games was likely to raise revenue.
18. B. 300. It was not the first hockey game on television, however. A game in England was broadcast two years earlier.

Did You Know?

The original Stanley Cup was only 7.28 inches tall.

CHAPTER 8:
THE 1940S

1. Which team went a record 23 games without a loss during a 48-game regular season on their way to the 1940–41 Stanley Cup?

    A. Boston Bruins
    B. Toronto Maple Leafs
    C. Detroit Red Wings
    D. New York Rangers

2. Though the Bruins nearly swept all of the awards in 1940–41, which goalie won the Vezina for his play with the Toronto Maple Leafs?

    A. Frank Brimsek
    B. Turk Broda
    C. Johnny Mowers
    D. Dave Kerr

3. Which team came back from a 3–0 deficit and won the next four games to win the 1941–42 Stanley Cup?

    A. Detroit Red Wings
    B. Montreal Canadiens
    C. Toronto Maple Leafs
    D. New York Rangers

4. Which player won the 1941–42 MVP playing for the Brooklyn Americans, a team that would not exist one season later?

    A. Bryan Hextall
    B. Sid Abel
    C. Lynn Patrick
    D. Tommy Anderson

5. In the first year of the "Original Six" era, which team won the 1942–43 Stanley Cup?

    A. Boston Bruins
    B. Detroit Red Wings
    C. Montreal Canadiens
    D. Toronto Maple Leafs

6. Because of World War II, the NHL stopped using what feature of the game during the 1942–43 regular season? It only returned in the 1983–84 season.

A. Overtime
   B. Penalty shots
   C. Suspensions
   D. Intermissions

7. The 1943–44 New York Rangers set an abysmal record by allowing an average of how many goals per game over the season?
   A. 4.43
   B. 5.18
   C. 5.80
   D. 6.20

8. Babe Pratt of which team was named the MVP during the 1943–44 regular season, though he was not in the top ten of scorers that season?
   A. Boston Bruins
   B. Chicago Black Hawks
   C. Toronto Maple Leafs
   D. Detroit Red Wings

9. Which player led the NHL in scoring and won the league MVP, but his team did not reach the Stanley Cup Finals?
   A. Maurice Richard
   B. Elmer Lach
   C. Toe Blake
   D. Bill Cowley

10. Which player became the first defenseman to score 20 goals in a season during the 1944–45 campaign?
    A. Bobby Orr
    B. Flash Hollett
    C. Earl Seibert
    D. Glen Harmon

11. During the 1945–46 season, which player was expelled from the NHL for betting on games?
    A. Gaye Stewart
    B. Bill Durnan
    C. Babe Pratt
    D. Max Bentley

12. The Montreal Canadiens lost how many games in the 1945–46 Playoffs on their way to the Stanley Cup?

    A. Zero
    B. One
    C. Two
    D. Three

13. During the 1946–47 season, the NHL began awarding the winning players of the All-Star game with how much money per player?

    A. $500
    B. $750
    C. $1,000
    D. $1,250

14. Maurice Richard broke which player's nose after losing a fight to rookie Gordie Howe?

    A. Alex Delvecchio
    B. Syd Howe
    C. Sid Abel
    D. Jack Stewart

15. What started happening after goals during the 1947–48 season?

    A. Players waving their arms in the air
    B. Players putting their sticks in the air
    C. Players doing creative celebrations
    D. Red lights behind the goal

16. During the 1947–48 season, Bud O'Connor won both the Hart Trophy and which other trophy?

    A. Art Ross Trophy
    B. Lady Byng Trophy
    C. Calder Memorial Trophy
    D. Vezina Trophy

17. According to a new rule beginning with the 1948–49 season, who could be a captain or alternate captain?

    A. Defenseman
    B. Coach
    C. Goalie
    D. Manager

18. A game at which arena was postponed on November 10, 1948, when a fog bank occurred over the ice, ruining visibility?
    A. Madison Square Garden
    B. Olympia Stadium
    C. Boston Garden
    D. Maple Leaf Gardens

Chapter 8 Answers:

1. A. Boston Bruins. They finished the season with 27 wins and 67 points, five ahead of Toronto for the best record in the league.
2. B. Turk Broda. He had a GAA of 2.00 and allowed 99 goals on the season. He just edged out Boston's Frank Brimsek, who had a GAA of 2.01 and allowed 102 goals on the season.
3. C. Toronto Maple Leafs. They completed what is called the "reverse sweep," winning four in a row after losing the first three, a rare feat in any sport with a seven-game series.
4. D. Tommy Anderson. He had 41 points and 64 penalty minutes in his 48 games with the team, though he did not lead the league in any scoring categories.
5. B. Detroit Red Wings. The league would not have more than six teams until 1967, some 25 years later.
6. A. Overtime. When overtime returned in 1983–84, they would reduce the time to five minutes and make it a sudden death format.
7. D. 6.20. In 50 games that season, the Rangers allowed 310 goals and only won six of those 50 games. They were 26 points behind the next closest team in the standings.
8. C. Toronto Maple Leafs. Pratt's defensive play likely helped Toronto make the playoffs, but they were quickly defeated by the eventual champions, the Montreal Canadiens.
9. B. Elmer Lach. He had a total of 80 points, with 26 goals. His teammate, Maurice Richard, had 50 goals in 50 games.
10. B. Flash Hollett. This record would be shattered by Bobby Orr decades later.
11. C. Babe Pratt. He appealed and was reinstated weeks later, missing nine games during the process.
12. B. One. They lost one game to the Boston Bruins in the Finals after sweeping Chicago in the semifinals.
13. C. $1,000. The award was an effort to give the All-Star game more meaning and get better performances from the players.
14. C. Sid Abel. Abel had taunted Richard, causing the retaliation after the fight. It marked the beginning of a big rivalry.
15. B. Players putting their sticks in the air. Red lights had been mandated in every rink just a couple of years prior.

16. B. Lady Byng Trophy. The trophy for excellence and sportsmanship indicates that O'Connor played a clean and gentlemanly game.
17. A. Defenseman. The rule was changed because goaltender Bill Durnan would use his captaincy to argue calls across the rink, giving his teammates more time to rest.
18. C. Boston Garden. The game was replayed the next night, and the Bruins beat the Red Wings 4–1.

Did You Know?

Connor McDavid is the youngest captain in NHL history. He was 19 when he got the "C" in 2016.

CHAPTER 9:
THE 1950S

1. Which team hired a hypnotist during the 1950-51 season to try and relax their slumping team's players?

    A. New York Rangers
    B. Chicago Black Hawks
    C. Boston Bruins
    D. Montreal Canadiens

2. Which two teams won all of the regular season trophies and awards but one, yet did not reach the 1951 Stanley Cup Finals?

    A. Rangers and Black Hawks
    B. Canadiens and Maple Leafs
    C. Bruins and Red Wings
    D. Rangers and Bruins

3. For the fourth straight season, which team finished with the league's best record at the conclusion of the 1951-52 season?

    A. Detroit Red Wings
    B. Chicago Black Hawks
    C. Boston Bruins
    D. Montreal Canadiens

4. Which American Hockey League team almost became the NHL's seventh team during the 1952-53 season?

    A. St. Louis Flyers
    B. Pittsburgh Hornets
    C. Cleveland Barons
    D. Providence Reds

5. Marguerite Ann Norris became the first female owner in the NHL, taking over which team for the 1952-53 season?

    A. New York Rangers
    B. Chicago Black Hawks
    C. Detroit Red Wings
    D. Montreal Canadiens

6. During this era, referees on the ice started wearing what color of uniform, instead of the cream color?

    A. Black and white stripes
    B. Orange

C. Green
   D. Yellow

7. Art Ross retired at the end of the 1953–54 season. Which team did he play for that was swept out of the 1954 playoffs?

   A. Detroit Red Wings
   B. Chicago Black Hawks
   C. Boston Bruins
   D. Montreal Canadiens

8. The Red Wings won Game 7 in overtime to take the 1954 Stanley Cup, beating which team 2-1?

   A. New York Rangers
   B. Chicago Black Hawks
   C. Boston Bruins
   D. Montreal Canadiens

9. Fans of which team rioted when their star player was suspended for the 1955 playoffs?

   A. Detroit Red Wings
   B. Chicago Black Hawks
   C. Boston Bruins
   D. Montreal Canadiens

10. Which player led the NHL in scoring for the 1954–55 season, though his team fell in the Stanley Cup Finals?

    A. Bernie Geoffrion
    B. Maurice Richard
    C. Jean Beliveau
    D. Earl Reibel

11. Before the 1955–56 season, NHL President Clarence Campbell wanted the penalty rule changed because which team was scoring multiple goals on single power plays?

    A. New York Rangers
    B. Chicago Black Hawks
    C. Boston Bruins
    D. Montreal Canadiens

12. Though Jacques Plante led the 1955–56 season in GAA, which goalie led the league with 12 shutouts?

    A. Glenn Hall
    B. Terry Sawchuk
    C. Harry Lumley
    D. Lorne Worsley

13. Which Red Wings player led the 1956–57 season in scoring, though his team could not win the Stanley Cup?

    A. Ted Lindsay
    B. Gordie Howe
    C. Norm Ullman
    D. Red Kelly

14. The Montreal Canadiens needed how many games to defeat the Boston Bruins and capture the 1957 Stanley Cup?

    A. Four
    B. Five
    C. Six
    D. Seven

15. Ted Lindsay and Doug Harvey are credited with the push for what in 1957?

    A. Bonus pay to coaches
    B. Curved sticks
    C. Players' union
    D. Mouthguards

16. Which player became the first to ever score 500 career goals during the 1957–58 season?

    A. Gordie Howe
    B. Ted Lindsay
    C. Maurice Richard
    D. Henri Richard

17. Which coach fined 14 players from his team $100 each for playing a terrible game on February 5, 1959?

    A. Toe Blake
    B. Rudy Pilous

C. Sid Abel
D. Punch Imlach

18. Which Rangers player won the Hart Trophy at the end of the 1958–59 season?

    A. Andy Bathgate
    B. Bill Gadsby
    C. George "Red" Sullivan
    D. Andy Hebenton

Chapter 9 Answers:

1. A. New York Rangers. When the team lost another game to Boston, the hypnotist said it was because they were not able to work with the Rangers goaltender.
2. C. Bruins and Red Wings. The only trophy they did not win was the Vezina, which went to Al Rollins of the Stanley Cup Champion Toronto Maple Leafs.
3. A. Detroit Red Wings. While those great finishes did not always lead to championships, it did in 1952.
4. C. Cleveland Barons. However, they could not come up with enough money to prove they could successfully participate in the league.
5. C. Detroit Red Wings. She took over after her father, James Norris, passed away at the age of 72.
6. B. Orange. It helped fans better distinguish between referees and some home-ice uniforms that had lots of white.
7. C. Boston Bruins. Art Ross had been the Bruins' manager since the team had begun playing in the NHL.
8. D. Montreal Canadiens. Floyd Curry scored for Montreal first, but it was Tony Leswick who got the overtime tally to win the Cup.
9. D. Montreal Canadiens. Rocket Richard was suspended for a violent altercation against a linesman.
10. Bernie Geoffrion. He had 38 goals and 37 assists for a total of 75 points, just one more than Maurice Richard, his teammate on the Canadiens.
11. D. Montreal Canadiens. The Canadiens were the only team to vote against the new rule, which allowed penalized players to leave the box after allowing a power play goal.
12. A. Glenn Hall. Hall's 2.10 GAA was second best to Plante's 1.86 that season.
13. B. Gordie Howe. He had 89 points on the season, four more than his teammate, Ted Lindsay.
14. B. Five. The Canadiens only lost Game 4 in that series before scoring a 5–1 victory in Game 5.
15. C. Players' union. The Red Wings owner stripped Lindsay of his captaincy and traded him to Chicago to intimidate players.

16. C. Maurice Richard. The award for most goals every season would eventually be named after this great player.
17. C. Sid Abel. His Red Wings lost 5–4 to the Rangers in a violent clash, hence the fines.
18. A. Andy Bathgate. He led his team with 88 points in 70 games, but the Rangers ended the season one point behind Toronto for the last spot in the playoffs.

Did You Know?

The first rink with artificially frozen ice was the Glaciairium, which opened in London, England in 1876.

CHAPTER 10:
THE 1960S

1. Gordie Howe became the first player in NHL history to reach what points milestone, which he did during the 1960–61 season?
   A. 800
   B. 900
   C. 1,000
   D. 1,100

2. Which trophy was retired and replaced before the start of the 1960–61 season?
   A. Hart Trophy
   B. Art Ross Trophy
   C. James Norris Memorial Trophy
   D. Vezina Trophy

3. Bobby Hull led the league in scoring during the 1961–62 season while playing for which team?
   A. New York Rangers
   B. Toronto Maple Leafs
   C. Chicago Black Hawks
   D. Boston Bruins

4. Which goaltender won the Hart Memorial Trophy during the 1961–62 season, a rare feat in the NHL?
   A. Johnny Bower
   B. Jacques Plante
   C. Glenn Hall
   D. Hank Bassen

5. Which coach was sued by a former referee after the coach accused the ref of handling a 1962–63 regular season game as though he had bet on the outcome?
   A. Punch Imlach
   B. Red Sullivan
   C. Milt Schmidt
   D. Toe Blake

6. Which team won the 1963 Stanley Cup by defeating the Detroit Red Wings in the Finals?
   A. Toronto Maple Leafs
   B. Chicago Black Hawks

C. Montreal Canadiens
   D. New York Rangers

7. Which team used the first overall pick in the first-ever amateur draft before the start of the 1963–64 season?

   A. New York Rangers
   B. Boston Bruins
   C. Detroit Red Wings
   D. Montreal Canadiens

8. Which team finished last in 1963 despite having six players in the All-Star game in October later that year?

   A. Chicago Black Hawks
   B. New York Rangers
   C. Boston Bruins
   D. Detroit Red Wings

9. Which player was the first recipient of the new Conn Smythe Trophy for playoffs MVP, after the 1964–65 season?

   A. Jean Beliveau
   B. Bobby Hull
   C. Stan Mikita
   D. Pierre Pilote

10. Which defenseman won his third straight Norris Trophy at the end of the 1964–65 season?

    A. Bill Gadsby
    B. Pierre Pilote
    C. Jacques Laperriere
    D. Carl Brewer

11. Which player was the Playoffs MVP in the 1965–66 playoffs, though his team did not win the Stanley Cup?

    A. Bobby Rousseau
    B. Stan Mikita
    C. Bobby Hull
    D. Roger Crozier

12. When the Red Wings' jerseys were stolen in Montreal before a January 1966 game, they had to get their farm team's jerseys express-shipped from which city?

    A. Halifax
    B. Toronto
    C. Hamilton
    D. Windsor

13. The 1966–67 season was the last to feature only six teams in the league. It was also the rookie year for which hockey legend?

    A. Bill Hay
    B. Bobby Orr
    C. Red Kelly
    D. Mickey Redmond

14. Which team finished with the league's best record for the first time ever at the end of the 1966–67 season?

    A. New York Rangers
    B. Chicago Black Hawks
    C. Boston Bruins
    D. Toronto Maple Leafs

15. Of the six new expansion teams to join the league in 1967–68, which one finished their first season with the best record?

    A. Philadelphia Flyers
    B. Los Angeles Kings
    C. St. Louis Blues
    D. Minnesota North Stars

16. Of the four expansion teams to make the 1967–68 playoffs, which one emerged to reach the Stanley Cup Finals?

    A. Philadelphia Flyers
    B. Los Angeles Kings
    C. St. Louis Blues
    D. Minnesota North Stars

17. Which player was the first in NHL history to score 100 points in a single season, which occurred during the 1968–69 season?

    A. Stan Mikita
    B. Gordie Howe

C. Bobby Hull
  D. Phil Esposito

18. In 1968, the NHL held its first of three Miss NHL Pageants. Which team's nominee won the first pageant?
    A. New York Rangers
    B. Minnesota North Stars
    C. Los Angeles Kings
    D. Oakland Seals

Chapter 10 Answers:

1. C. 1,000. Seven seasons later, Jean Beliveau would match Howe's feat.
2. A. Hart Trophy. The Hart Memorial Trophy replaced the old trophy, as its plaque had been deteriorating.
3. C. Chicago Black Hawks. Hull scored 50 goals in 70 games, and he tied in total points with Andy Bathgate of the Rangers with 84.
4. B. Jacques Plante. He also won the sixth of his seven Vezina Trophies that season.
5. D. Toe Blake. The league investigated and fined Blake $200, but the referee still resigned in protest.
6. A. Toronto Maple Leafs. They beat the Red Wings 4-1, including a 3-1 victory in Game 5.
7. D. Montreal Canadiens. They selected Garry Monahan with that pick, who would go on to play 12 seasons in the league.
8. C. Boston Bruins. The Bruins would finish the 1963-64 season in last place, too.
9. A. Jean Beliveau. His Montreal Canadiens defeated the Chicago Black Hawks in seven games to win the Stanley Cup.
10. B. Pierre Pilote. He was a big part of Chicago's success during his years with the team.
11. D. Roger Crozier. As the goaltender for the losing Red Wings, he helped his team through much of the playoffs.
12. C. Hamilton. The jerseys arrived on time, and the game started without any other issues.
13. B. Bobby Orr. He would go on to become one of the greatest defensemen in the history of the game.
14. B. Chicago Black Hawks. They finished with nine more wins than the Canadiens, but it didn't translate to playoff success.
15. A. Philadelphia Flyers. They finished the season one point ahead of the Kings for first place in the West Division.
16. C. St. Louis Blues. The Blues were quickly swept in four games by the Montreal Canadiens.
17. D. Phil Esposito. Though Hull and Howe also finished the season with more than 100 points, Esposito led the league that year with 126 points.

18. B. Minnesota North Stars. Lynn Marie Stewart won for the North Stars, and she received a new convertible car, a vacation, and a diamond watch set.

Did You Know?

Chris Chelios is the oldest player to win the Stanley Cup, at 46 years old.

CHAPTER 11:
THE 1970S

1. Which of these NHL teams was new to the league in 1970?

    A. California Golden Seals
    B. Pittsburgh Penguins
    C. Los Angeles Kings
    D. Buffalo Sabres

2. The NHL switched the playoff format to mix the divisions in earlier rounds because which team got swept three times in a row in the Finals?

    A. Philadelphia Flyers
    B. Los Angeles Kings
    C. St. Louis Blues
    D. Minnesota North Stars

3. Which Sabres rookie set a new rookie scoring record during the 1971-72 season?

    A. Marcel Dionne
    B. Ken Dryden
    C. Rick Martin
    D. Billy Smith

4. The 1972 Stanley Cup Finals concluded when which team beat the Rangers in six games?

    A. Boston Bruins
    B. Chicago Black Hawks
    C. St. Louis Blues
    D. Minnesota North Stars

5. Which player won the Conn Smythe, Norris, and Hart Memorial Trophies at the same time in 1972?

    A. Jean Ratelle
    B. Bobby Orr
    C. Brad Park
    D. Bill White

6. Which team moved into the Omni Coliseum at the beginning of the 1972-73 season?

    A. Atlanta Flames
    B. New York Islanders

C. Winnipeg Jets
   D. Miami Screaming Eagles

7. In February 1974, which 44-year-old defenseman died in a car accident?

   A. Gump Worsley
   B. Barry Ashbee
   C. Dean Prentice
   D. Tim Horton

8. Which team became the first expansion team to win the Stanley Cup in 1974?

   A. Atlanta Flames
   B. Los Angeles Kings
   C. Philadelphia Flyers
   D. St. Louis Blues

9. The Flyers repeated as champions in 1975, but who did they defeat in the Finals?

   A. Washington Capitals
   B. Kansas City Scouts
   C. Pittsburgh Penguins
   D. Buffalo Sabres

10. Which defenseman won his second Art Ross Trophy in 1975 and is still the only defenseman to ever win it?

    A. Denis Potvin
    B. Bobby Orr
    C. Guy Lapointe
    D. Borje Salming

11. The Philadelphia Flyers used which pick in the 1975 draft on the first Soviet-born and -trained player ever picked in the NHL?

    A. 110
    B. 130
    C. 140
    D. 160

12. Which team only won once in their final 44 games of the 1975–76 season?

A. Washington Capitals
   B. Kansas City Scouts
   C. New York Rangers
   D. Minnesota North Stars

13. The Kansas City Scouts moved to which city for play in the 1976-77 season?

    A. Seattle
    B. Cleveland
    C. Denver
    D. Ottawa

14. The Montreal Canadiens dominated the league again in 1976-77. They broke records in wins and points held by which team?

    A. Montreal Canadiens
    B. Boston Bruins
    C. Toronto Maple Leafs
    D. New York Rangers

15. Which Maple Leafs player became the first to score five goals on five shots?

    A. Kurt Walker
    B. Claire Alexander
    C. Brian Glennie
    D. Ian Turnbull

16. Which trophy made its debut at the conclusion of the 1977-78 season?

    A. Selke Trophy
    B. Art Ross Trophy
    C. Lady Byng Trophy
    D. Rocket Richard Trophy

17. The NHL required last names on jerseys beginning with the 1977-78 season. Which team protested by printing the letters in the same color as the jersey?

    A. Montreal Canadiens
    B. Toronto Maple Leafs
    C. Detroit Red Wings
    D. Chicago Black Hawks

18. Which team made the playoffs for the first time in 1977–78 but wouldn't do it again until 1988?
    A. Colorado Rockies
    B. Cleveland Barons
    C. Washington Capitals
    D. Vancouver Canucks

Chapter 11 Answers:

1. D. Buffalo Sabres. They did not make the playoffs that season, missing the cut-off by 19 points.
2. C. St. Louis Blues. The NHL hoped that mixing up the playoff format would lead to a more competitive Finals.
3. C. Rick Martin. Martin scored 44 goals that season, though he was not selected as the best rookie that year.
4. A. Boston Bruins. The Bruins finished off the series with a 3-0 shutout in Madison Square Garden, with the opening goal from Bobby Orr.
5. B. Bobby Orr. It was a dominant campaign by Orr, who changed how defense was played for the entire league.
6. A. Atlanta Flames. The Flames and the Islanders were starting their first seasons in the NHL that year, while the Jets and Eagles were participating in the World Hockey Association.
7. D. Tim Horton. Yes, it's the same Tim Horton as the chain of restaurants. The other three choices played their final NHL games during the 1973-74 season.
8. C. Philadelphia Flyers. They defeated the Boston Bruins in six games to claim their first Stanley Cup.
9. D. Buffalo Sabres. The Sabres, Flyers, and Canadiens had all finished the 1974-75 regular season with 113 points.
10. B. Bobby Orr. He scored 135 points in 80 games, and that included 46 goals.
11. D. 160. They selected Viktor Khatulev, though he never played a game for a North American team in his career.
12. B. Kansas City Scouts. They finished the season with 12 wins but didn't finish dead last. The Washington Capitals finished that season with 11 wins.
13. C. Denver. The team became the Colorado Rockies. Don't worry, because they would move again after six seasons.
14. A. Montreal Canadiens. They went on to sweep the Boston Bruins for another Stanley Cup victory.
15. D. Ian Turnbull. He would finish the 1976-77 season with 22 goals and 57 assists.
16. A. Selke Trophy. The trophy celebrates the best defensive forward, and the first winner was Bob Gainey of the Montreal Canadiens.

17. B. Toronto Maple Leafs. The team's owner thought names on jerseys would hurt sales of program pamphlets, which some fans would need to see which player corresponded with each number.
18. A. Colorado Rockies. Of course, they would no longer be the Rockies in 1988, but a different team in a different city by then.

Did You Know?

Joe Malone scored seven goals in a 1920 NHL game, the most of all time in one game by one player.

CHAPTER 12:
THE 1980S

1. Which player became the second in NHL history to score 50 goals in his first 50 games of a season during the 1980–81 campaign?

    A. Wayne Gretzky
    B. Butch Goring
    C. Mike Bossy
    D. Marcel Dionne

2. Which team kept their name when they moved to a new country for the 1980–81 season?

    A. Calgary Flames
    B. Vancouver Canucks
    C. New York Islanders
    D. Quebec Nordiques

3. The New York Islanders swept which team to win their third straight Stanley Cup in 1982?

    A. Chicago Black Hawks
    B. Los Angeles Kings
    C. St. Louis Blues
    D. Vancouver Canucks

4. Which team became the first in league history to wear long pants, which they did during the 1981–82 season?

    A. Winnipeg Jets
    B. Philadelphia Flyers
    C. Edmonton Oilers
    D. Quebec Nordiques

5. The city of Denver lost their hockey team before the 1982–83 season, and they wouldn't get another one until what year?

    A. 1994
    B. 1995
    C. 1996
    D. 1997

6. Which player was the last player from the Original Six era to ever play a game in the NHL, during the 1982–83 playoffs?

    A. Carol Vadnais
    B. Serge Savard

    C. Maurice Richard
    D. Wayne Cashman

7. Which player became the first American to be selected with the first overall pick, which took place during the 1984 NHL Entry Draft?

    A. Pat Lafontaine
    B. Tom Barrasso
    C. Brian Lawton
    D. Steve Yzerman

8. Which goaltender became the youngest to ever win the Vezina Trophy when he was given the award at the end of the 1983-84 season?

    A. Jim Carey
    B. Tom Barrasso
    C. Ron Hextall
    D. John Vanbiesbrouck

9. The Philadelphia Flyers lost to which team in the 1985 Stanley Cup Finals in five games?

    A. New York Islanders
    B. Pittsburgh Penguins
    C. Edmonton Oilers
    D. Chicago Black Hawks

10. Referees began wearing helmets for the first time during the 1984-85 season, but they wouldn't become required until which season?

    A. 2005-06
    B. 2006-07
    C. 2007-08
    D. 2008-09

11. Which NHL team was the first to win the Presidents' Trophy, which debuted for the 1985-86 season and is given to the team that has the best record at the end of each season?

    A. Edmonton Oilers
    B. Montreal Canadiens
    C. Calgary Flames
    D. Philadelphia Flyers

12. Which team lost their former Vezina-winning goaltender to a car crash on November 11, 1985?

    A. Edmonton Oilers
    B. Boston Bruins
    C. Philadelphia Flyers
    D. Pittsburgh Penguins

13. Which team changed their name, slightly, going into the 1986–87 season?

    A. Toronto Maple Leafs
    B. Detroit Red Wings
    C. Chicago Black Hawks
    D. Washington Capitals

14. Which Maple Leafs player needed more than 200 stitches when an ice skate cut his face on November 26, 1986?

    A. Borje Salming
    B. Wendel Clark
    C. Mats Sundin
    D. Tie Domi

15. Which player won the Hart Trophy after Wayne Gretzky missed more than a dozen games due to injury during the 1987–88 season?

    A. Pierre Turgeon
    B. Mario Lemieux
    C. Denis Savard
    D. Dale Hawerchuk

16. The 1988–89 Stanley Cup Finals was a matchup between the Montreal Canadiens and which team, who had won the Presidents' Trophy for the second year in a row?

    A. Calgary Flames
    B. Edmonton Oilers
    C. Washington Capitals
    D. Pittsburgh Penguins

17. In one of the most shocking trades in hockey history, Wayne Gretzky was traded from the Oilers to which team before the 1988–89 season?

A. Detroit Red Wings
   B. Los Angeles Kings
   C. New York Rangers
   D. St. Louis Blues

18. Which team lost to the Edmonton Oilers in the 1990 Stanley Cup Finals, falling in five games?

    A. Washington Capitals
    B. Montreal Canadiens
    C. Hartford Whalers
    D. Boston Bruins

Chapter 12 Answers:

1. C. Mike Bossy. He ended that season with 68 goals in 79 games, and his team also won the Stanley Cup.
2. A. Calgary Flames. They finished seventh in the league in their first year in Calgary, a successful start for their new home.
3. D. Vancouver Canucks. The Islanders also swept the Nordiques in the conference finals that season.
4. B. Philadelphia Flyers. The idea was that the players should have more speed from a more streamlined uniform.
5. B. 1995. Denver would get the Colorado Avalanche after watching their Rockies become the New Jersey Devils.
6. D. Wayne Cashman. His Boston Bruins were eliminated in the Wales Conference Finals, bringing an end to his career — and to an era.
7. C. Brian Lawton. Lafontaine was selected third, and Tom Barrasso was selected fifth. Steve Yzerman is not American but was selected fourth.
8. B. Tom Barrasso. He won the award during his rookie season, and he was only 18 years old at the time.
9. C. Edmonton Oilers. It was the second-straight championship for Gretzky and the Oilers.
10. B. 2006–07. Referee Andy Van Hellemond was the first referee to wear a helmet in the history of the league.
11. A. Edmonton Oilers. They had 56 wins during the season but could not win another Stanley Cup.
12. C. Philadelphia Flyers. Despite losing their goaltender in such a tragedy, the team still won their division and had the second-best record in the NHL.
13. C. Chicago Black Hawks. They went from Black Hawks to Blackhawks. Not a big change, but it was a departure from the original franchise documents.
14. A. Borje Salming. It was the third face injury of Salming's career. When he returned to play, he wore a protective visor on his helmet.
15. B. Mario Lemieux. Mario scored 168 points, including 70 goals, during his 77 games of the season.

16. A. Calgary Flames. The Flames won the Cup in six games, and as of 2024, this is the last time two Canadian teams faced off for the Stanley Cup.
17. B. Los Angeles Kings. Gretzky helped the Kings beat the Oilers in the first round of the playoffs that year, though the Kings were swept by the eventual champion Calgary Flames in the second round.
18. D. Boston Bruins. The Bruins swept the Capitals in the conference finals but couldn't overcome the star power of the Oilers.

Did You Know?

Garry Monahan was the first player drafted in the first-ever NHL Draft in 1963.

CHAPTER 13:
THE 1990S

1. Which player was named the league MVP for the 1990–91 season, though he finished second in scoring behind Gretzky?
   A. Mario Lemieux
   B. Adam Oates
   C. Mark Recchi
   D. Brett Hull

2. Which team won the 1990–91 Stanley Cup, defeating the Minnesota North Stars in six games?
   A. Pittsburgh Penguins
   B. Edmonton Oilers
   C. Boston Bruins
   D. Montreal Canadiens

3. The NHL added which new expansion team to begin the 1991–92 season, bringing the total number of teams to 22?
   A. Tampa Bay Lightning
   B. Ottawa Senators
   C. San Jose Sharks
   D. Florida Panthers

4. Which goaltender won his third Vezina Trophy in 1992, as he led the league in GAA and save percentage?
   A. Ed Belfour
   B. Patrick Roy
   C. Kirk McLean
   D. John Vanbiesbrouck

5. Which team won the Stanley Cup in 1993, marking the 100th anniversary of the trophy?
   A. Pittsburgh Penguins
   B. Los Angeles Kings
   C. Montreal Canadiens
   D. Boston Bruins

6. The San Jose Sharks won 11 games on the 84-game schedule of the 1992–93 season, one more win than which team, though they tied with 24 points in the final standings?
   A. Tampa Bay Lightning
   B. Hartford Whalers

C. Ottawa Senators
   D. Edmonton Oilers

7. Which player won the 1993–94 season MVP honors, as his team was the only one to average more than four goals per game?

   A. Steve Yzerman
   B. Sergei Fedorov
   C. Ray Sheppard
   D. Paul Coffey

8. Which team joined the NHL's Western Conference as an expansion team for the 1993–94 season?

   A. Mighty Ducks of Anaheim
   B. Florida Panthers
   C. Tampa Bay Lightning
   D. Ottawa Senators

9. Because of a lockout, each NHL team only played how many games in the 1994–95 regular season?

   A. 44
   B. 48
   C. 50
   D. 52

10. Eric Lindros and which player tied with 70 points each at the end of the 1994–95 season?

    A. Joe Sakic
    B. Alexei Zhamnov
    C. Jaromir Jagr
    D. Ron Francis

11. Which team moved to a new city for the 1995–96 season and went on to win the Stanley Cup?

    A. Colorado Avalanche
    B. Florida Panthers
    C. Winnipeg Jets
    D. Hartford Whalers

12. The 1995 NHL Entry Draft was the first to use a draft lottery. Who won the first overall pick?

A. New York Islanders
B. Los Angeles Kings
C. Mighty Ducks of Anaheim
D. Ottawa Senators

13. Which player was named the season MVP at the end of the 1996-97 season, though his team lost in the second round of the playoffs?

    A. Martin Brodeur
    B. Dominik Hasek
    C. Patrick Roy
    D. Mike Vernon

14. Which player was the last to use a helmet and played his final game at the end of the 1996-97 season?

    A. Dave McLlwain
    B. Dale Hawerchuk
    C. Craig MacTavish
    D. Tim Hunter

15. The Detroit Red Wings won the 1998 Stanley Cup despite losing which defenseman to a career-ending injury in a car accident?

    A. Vladimir Konstantinov
    B. Slava Kozlov
    C. Slava Fetisov
    D. Igor Larionov

16. The NHL approved four new franchises in the summer of 1997 to be added in the coming years. Which team joined first?

    A. Atlanta Thrashers
    B. Columbus Blue Jackets
    C. Minnesota Wild
    D. Nashville Predators

17. Which great player retired at the end of the 1998-99 season?

    A. Mario Lemieux
    B. Jaromir Jagr
    C. Wayne Gretzky
    D. Ed Belfour

18. Which team defeated the defending champion Dallas Stars to win the 1999–2000 Stanley Cup?
    A. Washington Capitals
    B. Montreal Canadiens
    C. New Jersey Devils
    D. Boston Bruins

Chapter 13 Answers:

1. D. Brett Hull. He scored 86 goals in 78 games that season, but St. Louis fell in the second round of the playoffs to Minnesota.
2. A. Pittsburgh Penguins. Mario Lemieux was named Playoffs MVP as the team captured its first Stanley Cup.
3. C. San Jose Sharks. The Sharks finished that season dead last, with 17 wins in 80 games, 13 points behind the Quebec Nordiques.
4. B. Patrick Roy. He had a save percentage of .914 and a GAA of 2.36. He also collected 36 wins out of 67 games played for the season.
5. C. Montreal Canadiens. The 1993 Stanley Cup, as of 2024, marks the last time a Canadian team has raised the trophy.
6. C. Ottawa Senators. It was a tough debut season for the new Ottawa team, but things would gradually improve for them.
7. B. Sergei Fedorov. However, his Detroit Red Wings were upset in the first round by the San Jose Sharks in seven games.
8. A. Mighty Ducks of Anaheim. The team had jerseys that matched the uniforms from the Disney movie titled *The Mighty Ducks*.
9. B. 48. The Detroit Red Wings finished with the best record in the shortened season, though they lost in the Stanley Cup Finals.
10. C. Jaromir Jagr. Jagr had 32 goals to Lindros' 29, but both players had dominant seasons.
11. A. Colorado Avalanche. They swept the Florida Panthers to win the Stanley Cup Finals, and Joe Sakic was named Playoffs MVP.
12. D. Ottawa Senators. The Senators selected Bryan Berard with the first pick, while Hall-of-Famer Jarome Iginla went 11th to the Dallas Stars.
13. B. Dominik Hasek. His .930 save percentage led the league, though he did not lead in GAA.
14. C. Craig MacTavish. He finished his career with the St. Louis Blues, who lost in the first round of the 1997 playoffs.
15. A. Vladimir Konstantinov. He was injured in an accident just days after the Red Wings had won the Cup in 1997, the year before.
16. D. Nashville Predators. They joined the NHL in 1998, followed by the Thrashers in 1999, and then the Blue Jackets and Wild in 2000.
17. C. Wayne Gretzky. Gretzky finished his career with the New York Rangers and remains, as of 2024, the NHL all-time points leader.

18. C. New Jersey Devils. They won the Finals series in six games, their second championship in six years.

Did You Know?

Brian Skrudland scored the fastest overtime goal in NHL Playoffs history in 1986 when he scored nine seconds into the overtime of Game 2 of the Stanley Cup Finals.

CHAPTER 14:
THE 2000S

1. The 2000–01 NHL season came to an end when the Colorado Avalanche helped which soon-to-be Hall of Fame defenseman raise the Stanley Cup for the first time in his 22-year career?

    A. Adam Foote
    B. Ray Bourque
    C. Rob Blake
    D. Greg de Vries

2. Which player returned from retirement on December 27, 2000, after being away for three and a half years? He scored in his first game back.

    A. Jaromir Jagr
    B. Wayne Gretzky
    C. Mario Lemieux
    D. Dino Ciccarelli

3. The NHL took a break from February 14 to February 25, 2002, for what?

    A. The September 11 attacks
    B. Players' strike
    C. Winter Olympics
    D. Civil protests

4. After a fan was killed by a deflected puck during the 2001–02 season, it became mandatory for every arena to have protective netting. In which team's arena did the incident occur?

    A. Calgary Flames
    B. Columbus Blue Jackets
    C. Atlanta Thrashers
    D. Minnesota Wild

5. Which power forward was selected first overall by the Columbus Blue Jackets in the 2002 NHL Entry Draft?

    A. Joffrey Lupul
    B. Scottie Upshall
    C. Chris Higgins
    D. Rick Nash

6. Which coach received the Jack Adams Award when he got the Minnesota Wild into their first playoff appearance in 2003?

    A. Paul Maurice
    B. John Tortorella
    C. Ken Hitchcock
    D. Jacques Lemaire

7. Which team won their first Stanley Cup in 2004, defeating the Calgary Flames in seven games?

    A. Ottawa Senators
    B. Vancouver Canucks
    C. Tampa Bay Lightning
    D. Florida Panthers

8. Which goalie had 38 wins in the 2003–04 season, with 11 of those wins being shutouts?

    A. Martin Brodeur
    B. Ed Belfour
    C. Marty Turco
    D. Tomas Vokoun

9. Which player was drafted first overall during the 2004 NHL Entry Draft?

    A. Evgeni Malkin
    B. Andrew Ladd
    C. Alexander Ovechkin
    D. Devan Dubnyk

10. The 2005–06 season began with many rule changes, including getting rid of what?

    A. Two-line pass offsides
    B. Shootouts
    C. Microphones on referees
    D. Double-minor penalties

11. In February 2006, it was revealed that which team's assistant coach, Rick Tocchet, was involved in an illegal sports gambling ring?

    A. San Jose Sharks
    B. Phoenix Coyotes

C. Colorado Avalanche
D. Los Angeles Kings

12. One year after being drafted, which player led the league in scoring for the 2006-07 season?

    A. Alexander Ovechkin
    B. Joe Thornton
    C. Vincent Lecavalier
    D. Sidney Crosby

13. Which team won the 2006-07 Stanley Cup, with their captain, Scott Niedermayer, being named Playoffs MVP?

    A. Anaheim Ducks
    B. Ottawa Senators
    C. Detroit Red Wings
    D. Dallas Stars

14. Which team won their fourth Presidents' Trophy of the decade when they won it in 2008?

    A. Ottawa Senators
    B. Buffalo Sabres
    C. Detroit Red Wings
    D. Washington Capitals

15. Alexander Ovechkin led the NHL in scoring for the 2007-08 season with 112 points and how many goals?

    A. 55
    B. 60
    C. 65
    D. 45

16. Which goaltender made the last-second save in Game 7 to win the 2009 Stanley Cup for his team?

    A. Chris Osgood
    B. Marc-Andre Fleury
    C. Dominik Hasek
    D. Henrik Lundqvist

17. Which team hosted the All-Star Game in January 2009 to celebrate their 100th season of hockey?

A. Toronto Maple Leafs
   B. Montreal Canadiens
   C. Ottawa Senators
   D. Boston Bruins

18. Which player scored the game-winning overtime goal in Game 6 of the 2010 Stanley Cup Finals to help his team raise the Stanley Cup?
    A. Jonathan Toews
    B. Patrick Sharp
    C. Andrew Ladd
    D. Patrick Kane

Chapter 14 Answers:

1. B. Ray Bourque. Bourque scored 59 points that season, and when his career was over, he had more points than any other defenseman in NHL history.
2. C. Mario Lemieux. He was a big help to Jaromir Jagr, who went on to win his fourth straight Art Ross Trophy.
3. C. Winter Olympics. Canada's Men's and Women's teams both won gold medals. US' Men's and Women's both won silver.
4. B. Columbus Blue Jackets. To this day, NHL arenas have protective netting behind both goals above the glass to protect from errant pucks.
5. D. Rick Nash. The big forward had a good career in the NHL, splitting seasons with the Blue Jackets, Rangers, and Bruins.
6. D. Jacques Lemaire. The Wild were expected to struggle, but Lemaire got the team into the playoffs as the sixth seed in the Western Conference.
7. C. Tampa Bay Lightning. A big help to the team was Martin St. Louis, who won the Art Ross Trophy that season.
8. A. Martin Brodeur. He had a save percentage of .917 that season, and he played 75 of his team's 82 games.
9. C. Alexander Ovechkin. He would have to wait to play in the NHL, though, because the 2004–05 season was lost to a labor dispute.
10. A. Two-line pass offsides. This allowed for more breakaways and a faster pace of play, hoping to increase entertainment value.
11. B. Phoenix Coyotes. There were also rumors that Wayne Gretzky's wife was involved, but no charges were filed against her.
12. D. Sidney Crosby. He collected 120 points in 79 games, including 84 assists. It was an early sign of the domination to come.
13. A. Anaheim Ducks. They defeated the Ottawa Senators in five games to win the Cup.
14. C. Detroit Red Wings. They would also win the 2008 Stanley Cup, just as they did in 2002.
15. C. 65. He also had 47 assists for a total of 112 points, six more than Evgeni Malkin.
16. B. Marc-Andre Fleury. He stopped a shot by Nicklas Lidstrom to win the Stanley Cup for the Pittsburgh Penguins.

17. B. Montreal Canadiens. The Canadiens barely made the playoffs after tying the Panthers in points but had the head-to-head tiebreaker. They were swept out of the first round.
18. D. Patrick Kane. Much of the arena did not know the puck had gone into the net as Kane celebrated with his teammates.

Did You Know?

Ron Tugnutt holds the NHL record of 70 saves in one NHL game, back in 1991.

CHAPTER 15:
THE 2010S

1. The 2010–11 season marked the final year for which team?

    A. Hartford Whalers
    B. Atlanta Thrashers
    C. Colorado Rockies
    D. Winnipeg Jets

2. Which team won the Presidents' Trophy for the 2010–11 season, but their playoff run ended in heartbreak?

    A. Montreal Canadiens
    B. Toronto Maple Leafs
    C. Vancouver Canucks
    D. Calgary Flames

3. When his team won the 2012 Stanley Cup, which player was named the Playoffs MVP for his great goaltending?

    A. Martin Brodeur
    B. Jonathan Quick
    C. Roberto Luongo
    D. Tim Thomas

4. Which player led the NHL in goals for the 2011–12 season with 60 goals?

    A. Evgeni Malkin
    B. James Neal
    C. Ilya Kovalchuk
    D. Steven Stamkos

5. The 2012–13 season was shortened to how many games per team because of a lockout?

    A. 44
    B. 48
    C. 52
    D. 56

6. The Blackhawks won another Stanley Cup in 2013. Which star was named the Playoffs MVP?

    A. Patrick Kane
    B. Jonathan Toews
    C. Duncan Keith
    D. Corey Crawford

7. Players with fewer than how many games of NHL experience were required to wear a visor beginning in the 2013-14 season?

    A. 15
    B. 20
    C. 25
    D. 30

8. The rules for which infraction were changed during the 2013-14 season to prevent players getting injured racing into the boards?

    A. Two-line pass
    B. Icing
    C. Delayed offsides
    D. Line changes

9. Which team's ten-year playoffs streak ended in the 2014-15 season?

    A. Buffalo Sabres
    B. Boston Bruins
    C. Los Angeles Kings
    D. San Jose Sharks

10. There were two Dallas Stars players in the top ten for scoring during the 2014-15 season, and one of them was Jamie Benn. Who was the other?

    A. Tyler Seguin
    B. Jason Spezza
    C. John Klingberg
    D. Cody Eakin

11. The 2015-16 San Jose Sharks recovered and made a deep run into the playoffs before losing to which team in the Finals?

    A. Washington Capitals
    B. Pittsburgh Penguins
    C. Florida Panthers
    D. Tampa Bay Lightning

12. Which of these players made their NHL debut during the 2015-16 season?

    A. Artemi Panarin
    B. Niklas Backstrom

    C. Shawn Horcoff
    D. Andrew Ference

13. The Penguins won the Stanley Cup again in 2017, becoming the first team to repeat as champions since which squad?

    A. Colorado Avalanche
    B. New Jersey Devils
    C. Detroit Red Wings
    D. Edmonton Oilers

14. Which player was selected first overall during the 2016 NHL Entry Draft?

    A. Tage Thompson
    B. Matthew Tkachuk
    C. Patrik Laine
    D. Auston Matthews

15. The Vegas Golden Knights debuted during the 2017–18 season, making it all the way to the Stanley Cup Finals, where they lost to which team?

    A. Washington Capitals
    B. Tampa Bay Lightning
    C. Boston Bruins
    D. Pittsburgh Penguins

16. The Los Angeles Kings and which team played two 2017–18 preseason games in Shanghai and Beijing, China, marking the first NHL games played in that country?

    A. San Jose Sharks
    B. Vegas Golden Knights
    C. Vancouver Canucks
    D. Winnipeg Jets

17. Which team picked Rasmus Dahlin with the first overall pick in the 2018 NHL Entry Draft?

    A. Vancouver Canucks
    B. Arizona Coyotes
    C. Anaheim Ducks
    D. Buffalo Sabres

18. Which team won their first-ever Stanley Cup in 2019?
    A. Columbus Blue Jackets
    B. St. Louis Blues
    C. Nashville Predators
    D. Winnipeg Jets

Chapter 15 Answers:

1. B. Atlanta Thrashers. The team would move to Winnipeg to become the new Jets team for the next season.
2. C. Vancouver Canucks. They had 117 points on the season, but they fell to the Boston Bruins in the Stanley Cup Finals.
3. B. Jonathan Quick. The Los Angeles Kings defeated the New Jersey Devils to win the Stanley Cup that season.
4. D. Steven Stamkos. Despite Stamkos' great season, the Tampa Bay Lightning did not make the playoffs that season.
5. B. 48. The Chicago Blackhawks won 36 games that season, winning the Presidents' Trophy on their way to the Stanley Cup.
6. A. Patrick Kane. He scored 19 points in 23 games for his team, including nine goals at even strength.
7. C. 25. If a player did not have that many games, they had to wear a visor. Of course, veterans could choose to wear one.
8. B. Icing. The new rule would end the play if the defenseman reached the hashmark first.
9. D. San Jose Sharks. They would finish third-to-last in the Western Conference that season, a significant drop-off from the previous ten seasons.
10. A. Tyler Seguin. Benn led the league with 87 points, and Seguin was seventh on the list with 77.
11. B. Pittsburgh Penguins. The Penguins defeated the Sharks in six games to win another Stanley Cup for captain Sidney Crosby.
12. A. Artemi Panarin. He debuted with the Chicago Blackhawks. The other choices in this question were playing their final seasons during the 2015-16 campaign.
13. C. Detroit Red Wings. The Wings won in 1997 and 1998, almost 20 years prior.
14. D. Auston Matthews. He became the captain of the Maple Leafs in August 2024.
15. A. Washington Capitals. Vegas had finished in first place in the Pacific Division, winning 51 games in their first season.
16. C. Vancouver Canucks. The Canucks would not make the playoffs that season, while the Kings claimed the first Western Conference Wild Card spot.

17. D. Buffalo Sabres. Dahlin was a runner-up for the Calder Memorial Trophy, which was awarded to Elias Pettersson.
18. B. St. Louis Blues. They defeated the Boston Bruins in seven games to claim the Stanley Cup.

Did You Know?

The 1979–80 Philadelphia Flyers went 35 games without a loss (25 wins and ten ties).

CHAPTER 16:
2020-2024

1. The 2020 Presidents' Trophy went to which Atlantic Division team?

    A. Tampa Bay Lightning
    B. Florida Panthers
    C. Boston Bruins
    D. Toronto Maple Leafs

2. Though the Bruins were the top seed in 2020, which team won the 2020 Stanley Cup?

    A. Tampa Bay Lightning
    B. Dallas Stars
    C. New York Islanders
    D. Vegas Golden Knights

3. Which player won the Art Ross and Hart Memorial Trophies in 2020?

    A. Connor McDavid
    B. Nathan MacKinnon
    C. Leon Draisaitl
    D. Artemi Panarin

4. The 2020 Vezina Trophy went to which goaltender, though he did not lead the league in GAA or save percentage?

    A. Andrei Vasilevskiy
    B. Connor Hellebuyck
    C. Jordan Binnington
    D. Tuukka Rask

5. Which player was selected first overall by the New York Rangers in the 2020 NHL Entry Draft?

    A. Alexis Lafreniere
    B. Quinton Byfield
    C. Tim Stutzle
    D. Lucas Raymond

6. Which player was named Playoffs MVP when Tampa Bay won the 2021 Stanley Cup?

    A. Steven Stamkos
    B. Andrei Vasilevskiy

C. Nikita Kucherov
   D. Victor Hedman

7. The 2021 Presidents' Trophy went to which team, who did not reach the Stanley Cup Finals?

   A. Colorado Avalanche
   B. Montreal Canadiens
   C. Dallas Stars
   D. Carolina Hurricanes

8. Which player led the league in scoring for the 2020–21 season, though he did not score the most goals?

   A. Leon Draisaitl
   B. Brad Marchand
   C. Connor McDavid
   D. Auston Matthews

9. The 2021–22 season was the first to return to 82 games after two shortened seasons because of what?

   A. Labor disputes
   B. Tariffs
   C. War in Ukraine
   D. COVID-19 pandemic

10. Which player was drafted first overall in the 2021 NHL Entry Draft?

    A. Owen Power
    B. Matty Beniers
    C. Mason McTavish
    D. Luke Hughes

11. The Colorado Avalanche won the 2022 Stanley Cup, and which player was named Playoffs MVP?

    A. Nathan MacKinnon
    B. Gabriel Landeskog
    C. Cale Makar
    D. Darcy Kuemper

12. The Seattle Kraken joined the league for the 2021-22 season, finishing ahead of only which team in the Western Conference playoff race?

    A. Chicago Blackhawks
    B. Arizona Coyotes
    C. Anaheim Ducks
    D. San Jose Sharks

13. 13. The Florida Panthers lost to which team in the 2023 Stanley Cup Finals, though they would return one season later?

    A. Vegas Golden Knights
    B. Colorado Avalanche
    C. Dallas Stars
    D. Edmonton Oilers

14. 14. Which player was drafted first overall during the 2022 NHL Entry Draft by the Montreal Canadiens?

    A. Shane Wright
    B. Juraj Slafkovsky
    C. Simon Nemec
    D. Logan Cooley

15. 15. Which team won the 2023 Presidents' Cup but was eliminated in the first round of the playoffs?

    A. Carolina Hurricanes
    B. Colorado Avalanche
    C. Boston Bruins
    D. Dallas Stars

16. 16. The 2023-24 season was the final season for which team?

    A. Arizona Coyotes
    B. St. Louis Blues
    C. Winnipeg Jets
    D. San Jose Sharks

17. 17. Which player led the 2023-24 season in scoring, but his team was eliminated in the first round of the playoffs?

    A. Auston Matthews
    B. Artemi Panarin

- C. Alexander Ovechkin
- D. Nikita Kucherov

18. 18. Which goalie led the 2023–24 season in GAA but did not win the Vezina Trophy?
    - A. Sergei Bobrovsky
    - B. Thatcher Demko
    - C. Pyotr Kochetkov
    - D. Connor Hellebuyck

Chapter 16 Answers:

1. C. Boston Bruins. They finished with a .714 winning percentage, well ahead of Tampa, who had a .657, good for second in the Eastern Conference.
2. A. Tampa Bay Lightning. They defeated Boston in the second round, then defeated the Stars in six games to win the Stanley Cup.
3. C. Leon Draisaitl. He scored 110 points to McDavid's 97 points, though the two often played together and assisted on each other's goals.
4. B. Connor Hellebuyck. He did lead the league with six shutouts, and he also faced more shots and made more saves than any other goalie that season.
5. A. Alexis Lafreniere. New York only had a 2.5% chance of winning the first pick in the lottery, but they did.
6. B. Andrei Vasilevskiy. He played all 23 games for the Lightning, with a gaudy save percentage of .937 and five shutouts.
7. A. Colorado Avalanche. They finished the 2020-21 season with 82 points, tied with Vegas but with more wins in regulation.
8. C. Connor McDavid. He had 105 points in 56 games, but his 33 goals were behind the 41 from Matthews.
9. D. COVID-19 pandemic. Teams had spent two shortened seasons playing in front of zero or very few fans every night.
10. A. Owen Power. He was drafted by the Buffalo Sabres after playing college hockey for the Michigan Wolverines.
11. C. Cale Makar. The defenseman had eight goals and 21 assists to lead the team with 29 total points.
12. B. Arizona Coyotes. The Kraken had 60 points to Arizona's 57, but the season was still disappointing.
13. A. Vegas Golden Knights. The Golden Knights defeated the Panthers in five games, winning the Cup only a few years after their entry into the league.
14. B. Juraj Slafkovsky. The Slovakian left winger went first ahead of Nemec, Cooley, and Wright.
15. C. Boston Bruins. They lost to the Florida Panthers in seven games.
16. A. Arizona Coyotes. The team finished their time in Arizona with 36 wins in 82 games.

17. D. Nikita Kucherov. He finished the season with 144 points in 81 games, four more points than Nathan MacKinnon.
18. C. Pyotr Kochetkov. He had a GAA of 2.33, but Hellebuyck's save percentage of .921 led the league and got him another Vezina.

Did You Know?

Lars-Erik Sjoberg was the first European-born captain of an NHL team when he led the Winnipeg Jets in 1979.

CHAPTER 17:
MERGERS, MOVERS, AND GROWTH

1. In 1920, which team became the Hamilton Tigers, marking the first time an NHL team had moved to another city?

    A. Montreal Wanderers
    B. Quebec Bulldogs
    C. Pittsburgh Pirates
    D. Philadelphia Quakers

2. The original Ottawa Senators moved to St. Louis in 1934. How many seasons did the St. Louis Eagles survive?

    A. One
    B. Two
    C. Three
    D. Four

3. The California Golden Seals lasted how many seasons before moving to Cleveland?

    A. Six
    B. Seven
    C. Eight
    D. Nine

4. The Cleveland Barons lasted two seasons, then merged with which team in 1978?

    A. Calgary Flames
    B. New Jersey Devils
    C. Quebec Nordiques
    D. Minnesota North Stars

5. The Kansas City Scouts became which team in 1976?

    A. Atlanta Flames
    B. Colorado Rockies
    C. Quebec Nordiques
    D. Winnipeg Jets

6. The Colorado Rockies moved again in 1982, becoming which team?

    A. Winnipeg Jets
    B. Phoenix Coyotes
    C. New Jersey Devils
    D. Calgary Flames

7. The Quebec Nordiques moved to which city that had already had a hockey team in the past?

    A. Denver
    B. Cleveland
    C. Calgary
    D. Toronto

8. The Winnipeg Jets lost their team to which city, which was a new scene for ice hockey?

    A. Oakland
    B. Reno
    C. Phoenix
    D. Albuquerque

9. How many times did the Hartford Whalers make the playoffs in 18 seasons before their move?

    A. Eight
    B. Nine
    C. Ten
    D. 11

10. The Hartford Whalers became which team further down the coast?

    A. Atlanta Thrashers
    B. Carolina Hurricanes
    C. Dallas Stars
    D. Seattle Kraken

11. The Atlanta Thrashers played 11 seasons but only made the playoffs once, in which year?

    A. 2003
    B. 2006
    C. 2007
    D. 2008

12. When the Atlanta Thrashers left Georgia in 2011, they became which team?

    A. Winnipeg Jets
    B. Seattle Kraken
    C. Utah Hockey Club
    D. Vegas Golden Knights

13. The Arizona Coyotes paused operations, but their assets went to which new team in 2024?

    A. Seattle Kraken
    B. Vegas Golden Knights
    C. Utah Hockey Club
    D. Quebec Nordiques

14. Which of these four moved or defunct teams did not have a winning percentage above .500?

    A. Ottawa Senators (1917–1934)
    B. Montreal Maroons
    C. Atlanta Flames
    D. Arizona Coyotes

15. Of all the moved/defunct teams, which one had the most playoff appearances?

    A. Montreal Maroons
    B. Minnesota North Stars
    C. Winnipeg Jets (1979–1996)
    D. Ottawa Senators (1917–1934)

16. In what year did the NHL and WHA merge?

    A. 1977
    B. 1978
    C. 1979
    D. 1980

17. Of the four WHA teams to merge into the NHL, which one had the best 1979–80 season?

    A. Edmonton Oilers
    B. Quebec Nordiques
    C. Winnipeg Jets
    D. Hartford Whalers

18. When the Ottawa Senators returned for the 1992–93 NHL season, they won how many road games?

    A. Four
    B. Three
    C. Two
    D. One

Chapter 17 Answers:

1. B. Quebec Bulldogs. The Tigers only lasted five seasons before going under.
2. A. One. They won 11 of 48 games in their only NHL season, and Ottawa would have to wait decades to get a team once more.
3. D. Nine. The Golden Seals made the playoffs twice in those nine seasons but did not win a championship.
4. D. Minnesota North Stars. The team remained there for 15 more seasons before moving.
5. B. Colorado Rockies. The Rockies only played for six seasons, making the playoffs once.
6. C. New Jersey Devils. The team in New Jersey was quite successful in the 1990s and 2000s, establishing the team's presence.
7. A. Denver. The Colorado Avalanche have enjoyed success since their move in 1995, including many Stanley Cup Championships.
8. C. Phoenix. The Phoenix Coyotes made the playoffs nine times in 27 seasons before their next move.
9. A. Eight. The team had a .438 winning percentage, which, though not that great, improved after their move.
10. B. Carolina Hurricanes. In Carolina, the team won a Stanley Cup in 2006 after reaching the Finals in 2002.
11. C. 2007. The Thrashers were quickly swept in the first round by the New York Rangers.
12. A. Winnipeg Jets. It seems like Jets fans will make sure the team does not leave this time around!
13. C. Utah Hockey Club. The Utah Club played their first NHL season in 2024–2025.
14. D. Arizona Coyotes. In 27 seasons, their winning percentage was .495.
15. B. Minnesota North Stars. In 26 seasons, they made the playoffs 17 times. Thankfully, most teams made the playoffs during that period of NHL history.
16. C. 1979. Not every WHA team came in the merger, but the best teams were invited into the NHL.
17. D. Hartford Whalers. They finished the season with 73 points, good for 14th in the league. Edmonton squeaked into the playoffs with 69 points.

18. D. One. They won one game out of their 42 road games. They beat the New York Islanders in game 81 of the season by a score of 5-3 for their first road win.

Did You Know?

Manon Rheaume was the first woman to play in the NHL. She played preseason games for the Tampa Bay Lightning in 1992.

CHAPTER 18:
THE WESTERN CONFERENCE

1. The Western Conference, under another name, was founded in what year?

   A. 1974
   B. 1976
   C. 1978
   D. 1980

2. When the Western Conference was first founded, it was named after which hockey ambassador?

   A. James Norris
   B. Clarence Campbell
   C. Frank Calder
   D. Art Ross

3. When the Campbell Conference was formed in 1974, which two divisions were included in it?

   A. Patrick and Norris
   B. Adams and Smythe
   C. Norris and Adams
   D. Patrick and Smythe

4. When the NHL merged with the WHA, which two teams joined the Campbell Conference?

   A. Whalers and Nordiques
   B. Oilers and Nordiques
   C. Jets and Oilers
   D. Jets and Whalers

5. The Campbell Conference swapped one of their divisions with the other conference in 1981. Which two were switched?

   A. Patrick and Norris
   B. Patrick and Adams
   C. Smythe and Norris
   D. Smythe and Adams

6. When the Quebec Nordiques left the league in 1995, which team was added to the Pacific Division of the Western Conference?

   A. Calgary Flames
   B. Los Angeles Kings

    C. San Jose Sharks
    D. Colorado Avalanche

7. In 1998, the Western Conference went from two divisions to three. What was the name of the division they added?

    A. Southeast
    B. Northwest
    C. Southwest
    D. Northeast

8. The Eastern Conference reached 15 teams before the Western Conference, but what year did the West reach 15 teams?

    A. 1999
    B. 2000
    C. 2001
    D. 2002

9. When the NHL realigned in 2013, the Western Conference had how many teams?

    A. 14
    B. 15
    C. 16
    D. 17

10. Since the Western Conference, or the Campbell Conference, formed in 1974, which team has won more conference championships than any other team, meaning they have reached the Stanley Cup Finals more than any other team from the conference?

    A. Chicago Blackhawks
    B. Detroit Red Wings
    C. Philadelphia Flyers
    D. Edmonton Oilers

11. Which of these teams has been the Western Conference Champions more than once?

    A. Anaheim Ducks
    B. Montreal Canadiens
    C. Nashville Predators
    D. San Jose Sharks

12. Which team is the most recent to win the Western Conference two years in a row, as of 2024?

    A. Chicago Blackhawks
    B. Detroit Red Wings
    C. Edmonton Oilers
    D. Dallas Stars

13. Which team joined the Western Conference in 2017 as the conference's 15th team?

    A. Winnipeg Jets
    B. Arizona Coyotes
    C. Vegas Golden Knights
    D. Seattle Kraken

14. When the Utah Hockey Club joined the NHL in 2024, they joined which division of the Western Conference?

    A. Pacific
    B. Southwest
    C. Central
    D. Northwest

15. The NHL's West Division, from 1967 to 1974, awarded the Clarence Campbell Bowl to the team with the best record in the division. It was the precursor to the Western Conference. Who won the West Division in its first year, 1967-68?

    A. St. Louis Blues
    B. Chicago Black Hawks
    C. Philadelphia Flyers
    D. New York Islanders

16. Before the Campbell Conference was formed in 1974, which team led all West Division teams with three division championships?

    A. St. Louis Blues
    B. Chicago Black Hawks
    C. Philadelphia Flyers
    D. New York Islanders

17. From 1974 to 1981, when the Clarence Campbell Bowl was presented to the winner of the division and not the team from the

conference who reached the Stanley Cup Finals, who won the most season championships?

A. St. Louis Blues
B. Chicago Black Hawks
C. Philadelphia Flyers
D. New York Islanders

18. Which two teams won the Western Conference and went on to win the Stanley Cup five out of six years beginning in 2010?

A. Vancouver and Los Angeles
B. Los Angeles and Chicago
C. Chicago and Colorado
D. Colorado and Dallas

Chapter 18 Answers:

1. A. 1974. It was briefly suspended for the COVID-19 pandemic but reinstated after the pandemic restrictions were lifted.
2. B. Clarence Campbell. Campbell was the NHL's third president, serving from 1946 to 1977.
3. D. Patrick and Smythe. The Patrick Division had the Flames, Islanders, Rangers, and Flyers. The Smythe Division had the Black Hawks, Scouts, North Stars, Blues, and Canucks.
4. C. Jets and Oilers. The teams were well suited geographically to be part of the Western Conference.
5. A. Patrick and Norris. Several teams were also shuffled in the divisions to reduce travel time for the entire league.
6. D. Colorado Avalanche. Of course, in their first year of existence, the Avalanche went on to win the Stanley Cup.
7. B. Northwest. The new division had four teams at the time of its inception: Calgary, Colorado, Edmonton, and Vancouver.
8. B. 2000. The Columbus Blue Jackets and Minnesota Wild both joined the league at the same time, bringing the Western Conference to 15 teams.
9. A. 14. The Columbus Blue Jackets and Detroit Red Wings were moved to the Eastern Conference, and the Winnipeg Jets were moved to the Western Conference.
10. D. Edmonton Oilers. They have won the conference eight times, and six of those wins took place from 1982 to 1990.
11. A. Anaheim Ducks. They have been the Western Conference champions twice, and the other three teams have been the champions once each.
12. B. Detroit Red Wings. In 2008 and 2009, Detroit played for the Stanley Cup, and no other Western Conference team has reached the Cup Finals two years in a row since then.
13. C. Vegas Golden Knights. They joined the Pacific Division and went on to represent the Western Conference in the Stanley Cup Finals.
14. C. Central. As of 2024, the league has four divisions of eight teams each and two divisions to each conference.
15. C. Philadelphia Flyers. The 1967–68 season was the first time the Clarence Campbell Bowl was awarded.

16. B. Chicago Black Hawks. They won the West Division three years in a row, from 1971 to 1973.
17. C. Philadelphia Flyers. They won it four times in those seven years, and the New York Islanders won the other three season crowns, not sharing the wealth with other teams.
18. B. Los Angeles and Chicago. They won four straight Stanley Cups for the Western Conference during that period.

Did You Know?

The most goals in one game by both teams happened in 1920 when the Canadiens beat the St. Patricks 14–7. The Oilers and Blackhawks tied that mark in 1985 with a 12–9 score.

CHAPTER 19:
THE EASTERN CONFERENCE

1. The Eastern Conference was originally named after which historic figure?

    A. Lord Stanley
    B. Prince of Wales
    C. King Edward VII
    D. Queen Elizabeth

2. The Prince of Wales donated the Prince of Wales Trophy to the NHL in what year?

    A. 1933
    B. 1939
    C. 1925
    D. 1930

3. When the Prince of Wales Trophy was first donated to the NHL, it was awarded to which team each year until 1927?

    A. American Division champion
    B. Most goals scored
    C. Best team GAA
    D. NHL playoffs champion

4. When the Prince of Wales Conference was formed in 1974, which new team joined the NHL as part of that conference?

    A. Kansas City Scouts
    B. Washington Capitals
    C. Pittsburgh Penguins
    D. California Golden Seals

5. The Wales Conference was split into two divisions, with which names attached to them?

    A. Adams and Norris
    B. Adams and Patrick
    C. Patrick and Norris
    D. Norris and Smythe

6. Which Wales Conference team moved to Cleveland before dissolving two years later?

    A. Washington Capitals
    B. California Golden Seals

C. Kansas City Scouts
   D. Cincinnati Cyclones

7. When the NHL and WHA merged in 1979, which two teams joined the Wales Conference?

   A. Whalers and Oilers
   B. Jets and Oilers
   C. Whalers and Nordiques
   D. Nordiques and Jets

8. In 1981, which team was moved from the Norris Division to the Adams Division?

   A. Montreal Canadiens
   B. Toronto Maple Leafs
   C. Hartford Whalers
   D. Quebec Nordiques

9. Which team moved from the Smythe Division to the Patrick Division of the Wales Conference in 1982?

   A. New Jersey Devils
   B. New York Islanders
   C. Pittsburgh Penguins
   D. Washington Capitals

10. The Wales Conference increased to 12 teams when which team joined in 1992?

    A. Quebec Nordiques
    B. Buffalo Sabres
    C. Ottawa Senators
    D. Washington Capitals

11. The Adams and Patrick Divisions were changed to which two divisions of the Eastern Conference in 1993?

    A. Northeast and Metropolitan
    B. Atlantic and Northeast
    C. Northeast and Southeast
    D. Southeast and Metropolitan

12. Which team joined the Atlantic Division of the Eastern Conference, and the NHL, in 1993, the same year as the Mighty Ducks of Anaheim?

- A. New Jersey Devils
- B. Ottawa Senators
- C. Tampa Bay Lightning
- D. Florida Panthers

13. The Eastern Conference split into three divisions in 1998. Which of these is not the name of one of those divisions?

    - A. Atlantic
    - B. Central
    - C. Northeast
    - D. Southeast

14. The Winnipeg Jets rejoined the NHL in 2011. Which Division of the Eastern Conference did they compete in during their first two seasons?

    - A. Southeast
    - B. Northeast
    - C. Atlantic
    - D. Central

15. The Eastern Conference was split into only two divisions starting in 2013. Which of these teams did not play in the Metropolitan Division in 2013-14?

    - A. New York Rangers
    - B. New York Islanders
    - C. Buffalo Sabres
    - D. Philadelphia Flyers

16. From 1938 to which year, the Prince of Wales Trophy was presented to the team with the best regular season record?

    - A. 1964
    - B. 1967
    - C. 1978
    - D. 1981

17. From 2020 to 2024, the Eastern Conference champions have all come from one state. Which one?

    - A. Pennsylvania
    - B. New York

C. Florida
D. Michigan

18. The Montreal Canadiens have been presented the Prince of Wales Trophy 25 times in league history, which is the most all-time. Who is second on the list?

    A. Detroit Red Wings
    B. Toronto Maple Leafs
    C. Pittsburgh Penguins
    D. Boston Bruins

Chapter 19 Answers:

1. B. Prince of Wales. Prince Edward donated a trophy to the league several decades before, earning him the honor of being remembered throughout hockey history.
2. C. 1925. It was not originally used as a trophy to designate the winner of one of the divisions in the league.
3. D. NHL playoffs champion. It was also awarded to the teams who had won the championship for the two previous seasons.
4. B. Washington Capitals. The Caps only won eight of their 80 games that season, so it was a rough start for the new squad, even with the top pick in the draft.
5. A. Adams and Norris. There were nine teams split between the two divisions, including the Capitals, who joined the Norris Division.
6. B. California Golden Seals. The Cleveland Barons, despite their new name and location, could not survive the 25- and 22-win seasons.
7. C. Whalers and Nordiques. The Quebec Nordiques joined the Adams Division, while the Hartford Whalers joined the Norris.
8. C. Hartford Whalers. It was part of a large realignment in the NHL to reduce travel times for teams.
9. A. New Jersey Devils. The team had relocated from Colorado, so they needed to play more teams along the East Coast.
10. C. Ottawa Senators. It had been decades since the city had an NHL team, so there was a lot of enthusiasm at the time.
11. B. Atlantic and Northeast. Both divisions had seven teams each, while the Western Conference teams had six teams each in their divisions.
12. D. Florida Panthers. They would reach the Stanley Cup Finals in 1996, only a few years after their inception.
13. B. Central. The Central Division is in the Western Conference, though it is the easternmost division in the West.
14. A. Southeast. It was not an ideal situation for the new team that had moved from Atlanta, but the league was not yet ready to realign the Conferences.
15. C. Buffalo Sabres. The Sabres were in the Atlantic Division of the Eastern Conference, not the Metropolitan.

16. B. 1967. Of course, during that time, the Original Six teams collected several of those trophies, although the Rangers and Black Hawks only got one each.
17. C. Florida. The Florida Panthers and Tampa Bay Lightning have combined to represent the Eastern Conference in the Stanley Cup Finals five straight years.
18. D. Boston Bruins. The Bruins have 18 trophies, the Red Wings have 13, and the Penguins have six. Toronto only has two because of the time they spent in the Western Conference.

Did You Know?

Victor Nechayev was the first Soviet player to play a game in the NHL, back in 1982–83, for the Los Angeles Kings.

CHAPTER 20:
THE METROPOLITAN DIVISION PART 1

1. Which NHL player has the most games played for the Carolina Hurricanes?

   A. Glen Wesley
   B. Eric Staal
   C. Ron Francis
   D. Jordan Staal

2. Which NHL goaltender leads all Carolina Hurricanes in wins?

   A. Arturs Irbe
   B. Cam Ward
   C. Mike Liut
   D. Sean Burke

3. Which Carolina Hurricanes player has had more shots on goal than any other?

   A. Eric Staal
   B. Ron Francis
   C. Jeff Skinner
   D. Kevin Dineen

4. As of 2024, which Hurricanes player has the team's best career plus/minus, at 158?

   A. Sebastian Aho
   B. Teuvo Teravainen
   C. Brett Pesce
   D. Jaccob Slavin

5. Which Hurricanes player has collected the most penalty minutes over their time with the team?

   A. Torrie Robertson
   B. Pat Verbeek
   C. Kevin Dineen
   D. Ulf Samuelsson

6. As of 2024, which NHL coach has the most wins with the Carolina Hurricanes?

   A. Rod Brind'Amour
   B. Paul Maurice
   C. Peter Laviolette
   D. Jack Evans

7. Which player has the most games wearing a Columbus Blue Jackets sweater as of 2024?

   A. Boone Jenner
   B. Rick Nash
   C. Cam Atkinson
   D. Nick Foligno

8. Which Blue Jackets player has the most goals in team history with 289?

   A. Nick Foligno
   B. Boone Jenner
   C. Cam Atkinson
   D. Rick Nash

9. When it comes to penalty minutes for the Blue Jackets, which player has the most?

   A. Jody Shelley
   B. Jared Boll
   C. Derek Dorsett
   D. Rick Nash

10. As of 2024, which Blue Jackets player has more shorthanded goals than any other?

    A. Rick Nash
    B. Gustav Nyquist
    C. Cam Atkinson
    D. David Vyborny

11. Which former Blue Jackets goaltender has the all-time most wins for the team?

    A. Steve Mason
    B. Sergei Bobrovsky
    C. Joonas Korpisalo
    D. Marc Denis

12. Which Blue Jackets coach leads the organization in wins?

    A. Todd Richards
    B. Ken Hitchcock
    C. John Tortorella
    D. Dave King

13. Which NHL player has the most games played for the New Jersey Devils?

    A. Martin Brodeur
    B. Ken Daneyko
    C. Patrik Elias
    D. Travis Zajac

14. Which New Jersey Devils player leads the organization in goals?

    A. Patrik Elias
    B. John MacLean
    C. Bobby Holik
    D. Travis Zajac

15. Which New Jersey Devils player leads the team in shorthanded goals, though it is a close race on the leaderboard?

    A. Patrik Elias
    B. Adam Henrique
    C. Travis Zajac
    D. John Madden

16. Martin Brodeur is far and away the Devils' leader in goaltender wins, but how many does he have?

    A. 588
    B. 688
    C. 866
    D. 855

17. Which New Jersey Devils coach leads the organization in wins?

    A. Jacques Lemaire
    B. John Hynes
    C. Lindy Ruff
    D. Peter DeBoer

18. Though Patrik Elias leads the Devils in goals, assists, and points, which Devils player is second on the team's all-time points list?

    A. Travis Zajac
    B. John MacLean
    C. Kirk Muller
    D. Scott Gomez

Chapter 20 Answers:

1. C. Ron Francis. Francis played 1,186 games with the organization, and the next closest player is Glen Wesley, with 913.
2. B. Cam Ward. His 318 wins put him well ahead of Irbe, who has 130 wins with the team. Only those four goaltenders listed as choices have more than 100 wins with the team.
3. A. Eric Staal. Staal collected 3,033 shots in his career, and Ron Francis is in second with 2,543.
4. D. Jaccob Slavin. He is well ahead of Sebastian Aho and Teuvo Teravainen, who are just over 100.
5. C. Kevin Dineen. He gathered 1,439 penalty minutes with the team, and Torrie Robertson is in second place with 1,368.
6. B. Paul Maurice. He spent 13 years with the team, and he won 384 games over that period, just less than 50%.
7. A. Boone Jenner. He passed Rick Nash, who had 674 games with the team before he moved on.
8. D. Rick Nash. He scored 289 goals in his 674 games, making him one of the first superstars in the team's history.
9. B. Jared Boll. He neared 1,200 penalty minutes, while Jody Shelley was just over 1,000.
10. C. Cam Atkinson. He already has 16, and Rick Nash is second with 14.
11. B. Sergei Bobrovsky. His 213 wins are more than double anyone else on the list, as Steve Mason sits in second place with 96.
12. C. John Tortorella. He spent six seasons with the team, amassing 227 wins with a .568-win percentage.
13. B. Ken Daneyko. He played 1,283 games for the organization, only 24 games more than Martin Brodeur.
14. A. Patrik Elias. He scored 408 goals, more than 50 ahead of John MacLean. Bobby Holik and Travis Zajac are forever tied with 202 goals.
15. D. John Madden. He has 17 shorthanded tallies, just one more than Patrik Elias. Adam Henrique is third on the list with 13.
16. B. 688. For reference, the next closest Devils goaltender is Chris Terreri, with 118 wins.

17. A. Jacques Lemaire. Lemaire was the Devils' coach for seven seasons, from 1994 to 2011. He won 276 games, 126 more than John Hynes, who is in second place on the list.
18. B. John MacLean. MacLean had 701 points, more than 300 points behind Elias but 150 ahead of Travis Zajac.

Did You Know?

As of 2024, Jon Cooper is the longest-tenured NHL coach.

CHAPTER 21:
THE METROPOLITAN DIVISION PART 2

1. Which New York Islanders player has more points than any other player in team history?

    A. Mike Bossy
    B. Denis Potvin
    C. Bryan Trottier
    D. Clark Gillies

2. Which Islanders goalie has almost double the wins of every other goaltender to ever wear the Islanders jersey?

    A. Billy Smith
    B. Glenn Resch
    C. Rick DiPietro
    D. Kelly Hrudey

3. Which legendary coach has more wins with the New York Islanders than any other coach in team history?

    A. Patrick Roy
    B. Jack Capuano
    C. Barry Trotz
    D. Al Arbour

4. Which New York Rangers player has more games played for the team than any other?

    A. Brian Leetch
    B. Rod Gilbert
    C. Harry Howell
    D. Ron Greschner

5. Which Rangers goalie has more wins than any other?

    A. Henrik Lundqvist
    B. Mike Richter
    C. Ed Giacomin
    D. Gump Worsley

6. When it comes to points scored, which New York Ranger has the most of any other player to wear the Rangers sweater?

    A. Brian Leetch
    B. Rod Gilbert
    C. Jean Ratelle
    D. Andy Bathgate

7. With the Rangers' long history, which coach won more games than any other on the list?

   A. Lester Patrick
   B. Alain Vigneault
   C. Emile Francis
   D. Frank Boucher

8. In Philadelphia Flyers history, which player is at the top of the list for games played in the orange sweater?

   A. Claude Giroux
   B. Bill Barber
   C. Sean Couturier
   D. Bobby Clarke

9. Bobby Clarke leads all Flyers in assists and points, but who leads the organization in goals?

   A. Bill Barber
   B. Tim Kerr
   C. Brian Propp
   D. John LeClair

10. Only two goaltenders in Flyers' history have won more than 200 games. Who has the most?

    A. Bernie Parent
    B. Steve Mason
    C. Carter Hart
    D. Ron Hextall

11. Which Flyers coach was on the bench for seven seasons in the 1970s and leads the organization in all-time wins?

    A. Mike Keenan
    B. Fred Shero
    C. Peter Laviolette
    D. Pat Quinn

12. The top three Pittsburgh Penguins' career leaders in games played are all active as of 2024. Which of these is not one of them?

    A. Brooks Orpik
    B. Sidney Crosby

- C. Evgeni Malkin
- D. Kris Letang

13. As of 2024, which Penguins legend leads in goals, assists, and points, with Sidney Crosby a close second in each category?

    - A. Evgeni Malkin
    - B. Jaromir Jagr
    - C. Ron Francis
    - D. Mario Lemieux

14. Which Penguins goaltender leads the team in all-time wins, losses, saves, and shutouts?

    - A. Tom Barrasso
    - B. Tristan Jarry
    - C. Marc-Andre Fleury
    - D. Matt Murray

15. Which Penguins coach has 382 wins in ten seasons, the all-time most for the organization?

    - A. Dan Bylsma
    - B. Eddie Johnston
    - C. Mike Sullivan
    - D. Michel Therrien

16. As of 2024, Washington Capitals' Alexander Ovechkin does not lead the team all-time in which of these categories?

    - A. Games played
    - B. Goals
    - C. Assists
    - D. Points

17. Which Capitals goaltender leads the team in all-time wins, losses, and saves and is tied for the most shutouts?

    - A. Olaf Kolzig
    - B. Braden Holtby
    - C. Don Beaupre
    - D. Al Jensen

18. Which Washington Capitals coach has more wins than any other and last coached a game for the team in 1990?

A. Barry Trotz
B. Bruce Boudreau
C. Ron Wilson
D. Bryan Murray

Chapter 21 Answers:

1. C. Bryan Trottier. He scored 1,353 points during his time with the team, ahead of Bossy and Potvin, who both had over 1,000 points with the organization.
2. A. Billy Smith. Smith had 304 wins from his time with New York, and Glenn Resch is second on the list with 157.
3. D. Al Arbour. In 20 seasons with the team, Arbour won 740 games, with a .568-win percentage. The next closest coach on the list is Jack Capuano, who won 227 games in seven seasons.
4. C. Harry Howell. His 1,160 games were 31 ahead of Brian Leetch. Howell, Leetch, and Rod Gilbert are all enshrined in the Hockey Hall of Fame.
5. A. Henrik Lundqvist. Lundqvist is the only Rangers goalie with more than 400 wins, at 459. Richter is second on the list with 301.
6. B. Rod Gilbert. He scored 1,021 points with the team, and he is the only player with more than 1,000 points. Mark Messier is fifth on the list with 691 points.
7. C. Emile Francis. Francis won 342 games over ten seasons with the team, good enough for a .602-win percentage.
8. D. Bobby Clarke. He played 1,144 games for the organization during his career. The next closest player is Claude Giroux, who played exactly 1,000 games for the team.
9. A. Bill Barber. He scored 420 goals for the organization, 51 more than Brian Propp. John LeClair is fifth all-time with 333 goals.
10. D. Ron Hextall. He won 240 games with the team, only nine more than Bernie Parent. Steve Mason is the only other Flyers goalie with more than 100 wins, as of 2024.
11. B. Fred Shero. He won 308 games with a dominant team that won the Stanley Cup. His win percentage was .642.
12. A. Brooks Orpik. Crosby leads the team all-time with 1,294 games. Malkin and Letang are both over 1,100 games, too.
13. D. Mario Lemieux. Lemieux's 690 goals, 1,033 assists, and 1,723 points are the all-time most for the Penguins, for now.
14. C. Marc-Andre Fleury. His 375 wins are 99 more than Barrasso, who is in second place.
15. C. Mike Sullivan. Sullivan has the most wins, but Bylsma left in 2014 with a .668-win percentage.

16. C. Assists. Ovechkin leads in the other categories easily, including over 1,400 games played and nearly 1,600 points.
17. A. Olaf Kolzig. He leads the team with 301 wins, 293 losses, and 18,013 saves, and he's tied with Braden Holtby as they both have 35 shutouts.
18. D. Bryan Murray. He won 343 games over nine seasons with the team, leaving with a .572-win percentage.

Did You Know?

In 1927, Elizabeth Graham of Queen's University was the first goaltender documented to use a mask in ice hockey.

CHAPTER 22:
THE ATLANTIC DIVISION PART 1

1. Which player leads the historic Boston Bruins in games played, assists, and points, as of 2024?

   A. Johnny Bucyk
   B. Ray Bourque
   C. Patrice Bergeron
   D. Don Sweeney

2. Which Boston Bruins player had 26 hat tricks throughout his career with the team, most by any Bruin?

   A. Johnny Bucyk
   B. David Pastrnak
   C. Cam Neely
   D. Phil Esposito

3. With a mark that might not ever be broken, which Bruins player ended his career with a plus/minus of 574?

   A. Ray Bourque
   B. Dallas Smith
   C. Bobby Orr
   D. Phil Esposito

4. Only one Bruins goaltender has ever passed 300 career wins with the team. Which of these was it?

   A. Tiny Thompson
   B. Frank Brimsek
   C. Gerry Cheevers
   D. Tuukka Rask

5. In the 100 years of Boston Bruins hockey, which coach has collected more wins than any other?

   A. Art Ross
   B. Bruce Cassidy
   C. Milt Schmidt
   D. Claude Julien

6. The Buffalo Sabres have played 54 seasons in the NHL, and which player leads the organization in games, goals, assists, and points?

   A. Craig Ramsay
   B. Gilbert Perreault

C. Mike Ramsay
D. Rob Ray

7. Which Buffalo Sabres player has 161 power play goals, the most by any Sabres player in the team's history?

    A. Rick Martin
    B. Thomas Vanek
    C. Dave Andreychuk
    D. Alexander Mogilny

8. Which Sabres goaltender leads the organization in wins and saves?

    A. Dominik Hasek
    B. Ryan Miller
    C. Don Edwards
    D. Martin Biron

9. Lindy Ruff has coached the Buffalo Sabres for 16 seasons and has almost 600 wins with the team. Who is second on the list for all-time wins?

    A. Scotty Bowman
    B. Floyd Smith
    C. John Muckler
    D. Don Granato

10. Which Detroit Red Wing player leads the organization in games played, goals, and points?

    A. Steve Yzerman
    B. Nicklas Lidstrom
    C. Gordie Howe
    D. Alex Delvecchio

11. Which Red Wings player leads the organization in all-time penalty minutes?

    A. Joe Kocur
    B. Bob Probert
    C. Gordie Howe
    D. Gerard Gallant

12. Which Red Wings goaltender leads the organization in all-time wins?

    A. Chris Osgood
    B. Jimmy Howard
    C. Harry Lumley
    D. Terry Sawchuk

13. Which Hall of Fame Red Wing player leads the organization in plus/minus, and it's not very close?

    A. Nicklas Lidstrom
    B. Sergei Fedorov
    C. Pavel Datsyuk
    D. Vladimir Konstantinov

14. Which Red Wings coach has the most wins among Red Wings coaches in the organization's history?

    A. Jack Adams
    B. Scotty Bowman
    C. Mike Babcock
    D. Sid Abel

15. Which Florida Panthers player already leads the team in all-time games played, goals, assists, and points?

    A. Aaron Ekblad
    B. Jonathan Huberdeau
    C. Stephen Weiss
    D. Aleksander Barkov

16. Which Panthers goaltender is the only one to have more than 200 wins with the team?

    A. Roberto Luongo
    B. Sergei Bobrovsky
    C. John Vanbiesbrouck
    D. Tomas Vokoun

17. Which Panthers player was on the team from 1993 to 2002 and leads the organization in penalty minutes?

    A. Peter Worrell
    B. Paul Laus

C. Scott Mellanby
D. Ed Jovanovski

18. Paul Maurice is going to pass which coach, who led the team in all-time wins through the 2023–24 season?

A. Jacques Martin
B. Peter DeBoer
C. Gerard Gallant
D. Doug MacLean

Chapter 22 Answers:

1. B. Ray Bourque. He played 1,518 games for the team, collecting 1,111 assists and 1,506 points on his way to the Hall of Fame.
2. D. Phil Esposito. His 26 hat tricks are nine more than Pastrnak.
3. C. Bobby Orr. He dominated the play for many years, and the plus/minus stat is an example of that dominance.
4. D. Tuukka Rask. He has 308 wins with the team, as of 2024. Tiny Thompson has 252 wins, and Brimsek is third with 230.
5. D. Claude Julien. He won 419 games over ten seasons as the team's coach, and he left the team in 2017 with a win percentage of .614.
6. B. Gilbert Perreault. He played 1,191 games, scoring 512 goals and collecting 814 assists in that span.
7. C. Dave Andreychuk. Andreychuk played 837 games with the team over his career and is now enshrined in the Hockey Hall of Fame.
8. B. Ryan Miller. His 284 wins are 50 more than Dominik Hasek, and Don Edwards is much further down the list, with 156 wins.
9. A. Scotty Bowman. He won 210 games with the team from 1980 to 1987, with a .594-win percentage. Ruff's win percentage, as of 2024, is at .559.
10. C. Gordie Howe. He played 1,687 games with the Red Wings, scoring 786 goals during those games.
11. B. Bob Probert. He collected 2,090 penalty minutes during his time with the Red Wings and was well-known as an enforcer on the ice.
12. D. Terry Sawchuk. He won 350 games with the team. Chris Osgood had 317 with Detroit, and Jimmy Howard is third with 246.
13. A. Nicklas Lidstrom. His 450 is well ahead of Fedorov, who is second at 276. Datsyuk is third with 249, and Vladimir Konstantinov is fourth at 185.
14. C. Mike Babcock. He won 458 games with the team over a span of ten years. Jack Adams had 413 wins in 20 years as the coach, and Scotty Bowman won 410 games in nine seasons.
15. D. Aleksander Barkov. He has more than 700 games with the team, 250+ goals and 450+ assists as his career with the team continues through 2024–25.

16. A. Roberto Luongo. He won 230 games with the team on his way to the Hall of Fame. Bobrovsky is second on the list with 150 wins.
17. B. Paul Laus. Laus had 1,702 penalty minutes with the Panthers, and second on the list is Worrell, with 1,375.
18. A. Jacques Martin. He won 110 games with the team in three seasons with a winning percentage of .520. Maurice has a winning percentage above .600 as of 2024.

Did You Know?

Howie Morenz died just over one month after breaking his leg during an NHL game in January 1937.

CHAPTER 23:
THE ATLANTIC DIVISION PART 2

1. Which Canadiens Hall of Fame player has more games with the organization than any other player?

    A. Henri Richard
    B. Larry Robinson
    C. Bob Gainey
    D. Jean Beliveau

2. Maurice Richard leads the Canadiens on the all-time goals list, but who leads in assists and points?

    A. Jean Beliveau
    B. Henri Richard
    C. Guy Lafleur
    D. Larry Robinson

3. Which Canadiens player leads in the all-time plus/minus category?

    A. Serge Savard
    B. Larry Robinson
    C. Guy Lafleur
    D. Steve Shutt

4. Which Canadiens goaltender leads the organization in all-time wins?

    A. Jacques Plante
    B. Patrick Roy
    C. Ken Dryden
    D. Carey Price

5. Which Canadiens coach has the most wins with the team, which he gathered during 13 seasons behind the bench?

    A. Toe Blake
    B. Dick Irvin
    C. Scotty Bowman
    D. Michel Therrien

6. When it comes to the modern Ottawa Senators, which player has more games wearing the sweater than anyone else?

    A. Daniel Alfredsson
    B. Chris Phillips

C. Chris Neil
   D. Wade Redden

7. Which Senators player leads the organization on the all-time goals, assists, and points lists?

   A. Daniel Alfredsson
   B. Jason Spezza
   C. Alexei Yashin
   D. Marian Hossa

8. Which goaltender is the only player to collect more than 200 wins with the Senators?

   A. Patrick Lalime
   B. Ron Tugnutt
   C. Ray Emery
   D. Craig Anderson

9. Which coach is at the top of the list when it comes to wins with the Senators?

   A. D.J. Smith
   B. Paul MacLean
   C. Jacques Martin
   D. Bryan Murray

10. Which Tampa Bay Lightning player leads the organization in games played, goals, and points?

    A. Vincent Lecavalier
    B. Martin St. Louis
    C. Steven Stamkos
    D. Victor Hedman

11. Which talented Tampa Bay Lightning player leads the team in all-time assists and shorthanded goals?

    A. Vincent Lecavalier
    B. Martin St. Louis
    C. Tyler Johnson
    D. Nikita Kucherov

12. Which incredible goaltender leads the Tampa Bay Lightning in almost every stat category and crossed 300 wins during the 2024-25 season?

    A. Andrei Vasilevskiy
    B. Ben Bishop
    C. Nikolai Khabibulin
    D. Daren Puppa

13. As of 2024, which coach leads the Tampa Bay Lightning organization in all-time wins?

    A. John Tortorella
    B. Terry Crisp
    C. Jon Cooper
    D. Guy Boucher

14. Only five Toronto Maple Leafs have played more than 1,000 games with the team. Which player played the most?

    A. Tim Horton
    B. Borje Salming
    C. George Armstrong
    D. Dave Keon

15. As of 2024, only one Maple Leafs player has more than 400 goals with the team, though Auston Matthews may join him soon. Who is that one player?

    A. Darryl Sittler
    B. Mats Sundin
    C. Dave Keon
    D. Ron Ellis

16. Which NHL enforcer had more than 2,000 penalty minutes with the Maple Leafs?

    A. Tiger Williams
    B. Wendel Clark
    C. Tim Horton
    D. Tie Domi

17. Which Hall of Fame goaltender is the only Toronto Maple Leaf to win 300 games with the team?

    A. Turk Broda
    B. Johnny Bower
    C. Felix Potvin
    D. Frederik Andersen

18. Which Maple Leafs coach has the most wins in team history, though he does not have the best win percentage among Leafs coaches?
    A. Pat Quinn
    B. Hap Day
    C. Punch Imlach
    D. Dick Irvin

Chapter 23 Answers:

1. A. Henri Richard. He played 1,258 games with the team. All four of the options in this question have more than 1,100 games with the team, and they are all in the Hall of Fame.
2. C. Guy Lafleur. He had 728 assists and 1,246 points in the 961 games he played with the organization.
3. B. Larry Robinson. Robinson's plus/minus sits at 692, 195 ahead of Serge Savard. Of the top ten Canadiens in plus/minus, eight of them are in the Hockey Hall of Fame.
4. D. Carey Price. He won 361 games for the team, and Plante is second on the list with 314.
5. A. Toe Blake. He won 500 games with the team, winning .634 of the points available. Irvin and Bowman both won more than 400 games with the team, too.
6. B. Chris Phillips. He played 1,179 games with the team, only one more game than Alfredsson.
7. A. Daniel Alfredsson. In his 1,178 games, he scored 426 goals and 682 assists for 1,108 points. The next closest player is Jason Spezza, with 687 points.
8. D. Craig Anderson. He won 202 games with the team, and Patrick Lalime is second on the list with 146 wins.
9. C. Jacques Martin. He won 367 games with the team from 1996 to 2024, where he coached two different stints for ten total seasons.
10. C. Steven Stamkos. He played 1,082 games and scored 555 goals. He also collected more than 1,137 points during his time in the organization.
11. B. Martin St. Louis. He had 588 assists for the team, and his 28 shorthanded goals are more than double the next closest player on the list.
12. A. Andrei Vasilevskiy. Besides his 300+ wins, he already has more than 35 shutouts, more than double the next closest Lightning goaltender.
13. C. Jon Cooper. He has more than 500 wins with the team, with a winning percentage well over .600.
14. C. George Armstrong. He played 1,188 games with the team, only four more than Tim Horton.

15. B. Mats Sundin. Sundin scored 420 goals in 981 games with the organization. Sittler has 389 goals, and Matthews is likely to catch those two in the next few years.
16. D. Tie Domi. He had 2,265 penalty minutes, and the next closest player, Williams, only had 1,670 minutes.
17. A. Turk Broda. Broda won 304 games with the team, and the next closest goaltender on the list is Johnny Bower, who won 219 games.
18. C. Punch Imlach. Imlach won 370 games behind the bench. He coached 12 seasons from 1959 to 1980 in a couple of different stints.

Did You Know?

The 1996–97 Detroit Red Wings ended a 42-year Stanley Cup drought with their sweep of the Philadelphia Flyers.

CHAPTER 24:
THE CENTRAL DIVISION PART 1

1. The Chicago Blackhawks have played almost 100 seasons in the NHL. Which player has the most games in the team's sweater?

    A. Stan Mikita
    B. Duncan Keith
    C. Patrick Kane
    D. Brent Seabrook

2. When it comes to goals, which NHL player has scored more than 600 goals for the Blackhawks?

    A. Stan Mikita
    B. Bobby Hull
    C. Patrick Kane
    D. Steve Larmer

3. Which Blackhawks leader has the most penalty minutes in the organization's history?

    A. Keith Magnuson
    B. Al Secord
    C. Dave Manson
    D. Chris Chelios

4. One Blackhawks goaltender has more than 400 wins with the team. Who is it?

    A. Glenn Hall
    B. Corey Crawford
    C. Tony Esposito
    D. Ed Belfour

5. Behind the bench, which Blackhawks coach has more wins than any other?

    A. Billy Reay
    B. Joel Quenneville
    C. Bob Pulford
    D. Rudy Pilous

6. Which Hall of Fame player leads all Colorado Avalanche players in games played with the team?

    A. Adam Foote
    B. Milan Hejduk

C. Joe Sakic
  D. Michel Goulet

7. As of 2024, which Colorado Avalanche Hall of Fame player leads the organization in plus/minus?

   A. Nathan MacKinnon
   B. Devon Toews
   C. Alex Tanguay
   D. Peter Forsberg

8. Which Hall of Fame Colorado Avalanche goaltender leads the organization in wins but not in losses?

   A. Semyon Varlamov
   B. Patrick Roy
   C. Dan Bouchard
   D. Peter Budaj

9. Which Colorado Avalanche coach has the most wins in team history?

   A. Jared Bednar
   B. Michel Bergeron
   C. Bob Hartley
   D. Marc Crawford

10. The Dallas Stars have played almost 60 NHL seasons. Which player has the most games played, along with the most goals, assists, and points?

    A. Jamie Benn
    B. Neal Broten
    C. Mike Modano
    D. Jere Lehtinen

11. Which Stars player leads the organization in all-time penalty minutes with a lead of more than 300?

    A. Basil McRae
    B. Shane Churla
    C. Derian Hatcher
    D. Brenden Morrow

12. When it comes to plus/minus, which Stars player leads the organization by a margin of more than 50?

    A. Sergei Zubov
    B. Esa Lindell
    C. Mike Modano
    D. Jere Lehtinen

13. Which Stars goaltender leads the organization in wins and shutouts but does not lead in losses, shots, and saves?

    A. Marty Turco
    B. Kari Lehtonen
    C. Ed Belfour
    D. Cesare Maniago

14. The Dallas Stars have had many great coaches, but which one leads the team in all-time wins, as of 2024?

    A. Dave Tippett
    B. Glen Sonmor
    C. Ken Hitchcock
    D. Lindy Ruff

15. The Minnesota Wild have been in the NHL for 24 seasons, and which player has worn the sweater for more games than any other player?

    A. Nick Schultz
    B. Jared Spurgeon
    C. Mikko Koivu
    D. Jonas Brodin

16. The Minnesota Wild's all-time leading goal scorer has 219 goals for the team. Who is it?

    A. Mikko Koivu
    B. Marian Gaborik
    C. Zach Parise
    D. Kirill Kaprizov

17. Which Minnesota Wild goaltender leads the organization in all-time wins, as well as losses, goals against, shots, shutouts, and saves?

- A. Dwayne Roloson
- B. Devan Dubnyk
- C. Niklas Backstrom
- D. Manny Fernandez

18. The Minnesota Wild has had seven coaches in its history. Which one has the most wins?
    - A. Dean Evason
    - B. Bruce Boudreau
    - C. Mike Yeo
    - D. Jacques Lemaire

Chapter 24 Answers:

1. A. Stan Mikita. He played 1,396 games for the Blackhawks organization, while Keith, Kane, and Seabrook have played over 1,100 games with the team.
2. B. Bobby Hull. He scored 604 goals in 1,036 games with the team. Stan Mikita is in second with 541 goals.
3. D. Chris Chelios. He gathered 1,495 penalty minutes during his career with the team.
4. C. Tony Esposito. He won 418 games with the team and also leads with 302 losses and 74 career shutouts.
5. A. Billy Reay. He coached the team for 14 seasons, from 1964 to 1977, collecting 516 wins in that timeframe.
6. C. Joe Sakic. He played 1,378 games with the team, and as of 2024, leads the organization in all-time goals, assists, and points.
7. D. Peter Forsberg. His plus/minus is 210, but MacKinnon is in second place with 152. Could MacKinnon catch Forsberg before his career comes to an end?
8. B. Patrick Roy. Roy won 262 games with the team before retiring, while Varlamov has over 150 losses with the team. Roy only had 140 losses.
9. A. Jared Bednar. Through nine seasons with the team and counting, Bednar has more than 350 wins. Bergeron is second on the list with 265 wins from the 1980s.
10. C. Mike Modano. He played 1,459 games with the organization, scoring 557 goals and 802 assists during his career.
11. B. Shane Churla. He collected 1,883 minutes during his time with the organization, and Basil McRae has 1,567 minutes.
12. D. Jere Lehtinen. His 176 is the best in the organization's history, and Mike Modano is second with 118. Lindell, Zubov, and Brenden Morrow are all above 100 as well.
13. A. Marty Turco. He won 262 games with the team. Maniago leads the organization with 190 losses.
14. C. Ken Hitchcock. He won 319 games in eight seasons with the organization, and Tippett is in second place with 271 wins in six seasons.
15. C. Mikko Koivu. He played 1,028 games for the team and leads the organization in assists and points.

16. B. Marian Gaborik. Gaborik scored 14 goals more than Mikko Koivu, who scored six more goals than Zach Parise.
17. C. Niklas Backstrom. He won 194 games for the team, losing 142. His 28 shutouts are also the most by any Wild goaltender.
18. D. Jacques Lemaire. He won 293 games over eight seasons with the team. Mike Yeo is second on the list with 173 wins, and his winning percentage was slightly better than Lemaire's.

Did You Know?

In January 2008, the NHL had its first Winter Classic game between the Pittsburgh Penguins and Buffalo Sabres.

CHAPTER 25:
THE CENTRAL DIVISION PART 2

1. The Nashville Predators have 26 seasons in the NHL. Which player, as of 2024, leads the organization in games played?

    A. Roman Josi
    B. Shea Weber
    C. David Legwand
    D. Martin Erat

2. Which Nashville Predators player leads the organization in all-time goals scored and is likely to break the 300-goal mark during the 2024–25 season?

    A. David Legwand
    B. Filip Forsberg
    C. Roman Josi
    D. Shea Weber

3. Which Nashville Predators player leads the team in all-time penalty minutes?

    A. Jordin Tootoo
    B. Scott Hartnell
    C. Shea Weber
    D. David Legwand

4. When it comes to goaltending, which Nashville Predators goaltender has more wins than any other Predators netminder?

    A. Juuse Saros
    B. Tomas Vokoun
    C. Mike Dunham
    D. Pekka Rinne

5. In the 25 seasons the Nashville Predators have completed through 2024, they've made the playoffs how many times?

    A. 14
    B. 15
    C. 16
    D. 17

6. No St. Louis Blues skater has played more games in the team's sweater than which player?

    A. Barret Jackman
    B. Bernie Federko

C. Brian Sutter
D. Alexander Steen

7. Which Blues player has scored more goals in the team's uniform than any other ever to wear it?

A. Brett Hull
B. Bernie Federko
C. Brian Sutter
D. Garry Unger

8. Which St. Louis Blues player leads the team in all-time plus/minus?

A. Al MacInnis
B. Pavol Demitra
C. Paul Cavallini
D. Chris Pronger

9. Before the 2024–25 season began, which goaltender led the St. Louis Blues in all-time wins?

A. Jordan Binnington
B. Jake Allen
C. Mike Liut
D. Curtis Joseph

10. Which St. Louis Blues coach leads the organization with 307 wins?

A. Ken Hitchcock
B. Joel Quenneville
C. Craig Berube
D. Brian Sutter

11. The Utah Hockey Club began operations during the 2024–25 season. Who served as their first captain?

A. Dylan Guenther
B. Clayton Keller
C. Logan Cooley
D. Nick Schmaltz

12. Which Utah Hockey Club player scored the first goal in the team's history on October 8, 2024?

A. Dylan Guenther
B. Clayton Keller

C. Logan Cooley
   D. Nick Schmaltz

13. Which player was selected sixth overall by the Utah Hockey Club with their first-ever draft pick?

   A. Beckett Sennecke
   B. Cayden Lindstrom
   C. Ivan Demidov
   D. Tij Iginla

14. The Winnipeg Jets have participated in 24 NHL seasons. How many times have they made the playoffs before the 2024–25 season?

   A. Seven
   B. Eight
   C. Nine
   D. Ten

15. When it comes to games played for the Winnipeg Jets, which player is at the top of the list, quickly approaching 900 games?

   A. Bryan Little
   B. Mark Scheifele
   C. Blake Wheeler
   D. Adam Lowry

16. Though he is likely to be overtaken during the 2024–25 season, which player leads the Jets in all-time goals as of 2024?

   A. Mark Scheifele
   B. Ilya Kovalchuk
   C. Blake Wheeler
   D. Kyle Connor

17. Which Jets goaltender leads the organization with 40 (and counting) shutouts?

   A. Connor Hellebuyck
   B. Ondrej Pavelec
   C. Kari Lehtonen
   D. Milan Hnilicka

18. Which Winnipeg Jets coach has more than 300 wins, while the next closest coach only has 136?
    A. Rick Bowness
    B. Bob Hartley
    C. Claude Noel
    D. Paul Maurice

Chapter 25 Answers:

1. C. David Legwand. He played 956 games for the team during his career, but he is likely to be surpassed by Roman Josi during the 2024–25 season.
2. B. Filip Forsberg. As Forsberg nears 300 goals, Legwand, Josi, and Weber are next on the scoring list.
3. A. Jordin Tootoo. His 725 penalty minutes may not seem like very many, but in today's NHL, that might remain at the top of the list for a very long time.
4. D. Pekka Rinne. Rinne won 369 games while losing 213. He also leads the organization with 60 shutouts.
5. C. 16. Many of those appearances are thanks to the great coaches the team has had. All four coaches in team history have a win percentage above .500. Barry Trotz won 557 games in 15 seasons.
6. B. Bernie Federko. He played 927 games with the team in his career and leads in all-time assists and points.
7. A. Brett Hull. Hull scored 527 goals for the team in his 744 career games. He is the only Blues player with more than 400 goals in a career with the team.
8. D. Chris Pronger. Pronger's 140 is the best in team history, followed closely by MacInnis' 132. Cavallini and Demitra are next on the list, tied at 99.
9. C. Mike Liut. He had 151 wins with the team during his career, but Binnington is likely to overtake him during the 2024–25 season.
10. B. Joel Quenneville. He coached the team from 1997 to 2004, for a total of eight seasons. He is the only coach, out of the 28 in team history, to win 300 games.
11. B. Clayton Keller. He was named the team's captain on October 4, 2024.
12. A. Dylan Guenther. He scored the team's first goal during a game against the Chicago Blackhawks.
13. D. Tij Iginla. The Utah Hockey Club also selected Cole Beaudoin with the 24th overall pick in the first round.
14. B. Eight. The Jets have reached the playoffs eight times, with a record of 18–35 during those appearances.

15. C. Blake Wheeler. Going into the 2024–25 season, he is expected to be the first Jets player in history to play 900 games for the team.
16. B. Ilya Kovalchuk. His 328 goals lead the organization, but he is closely trailed by Schiefele, Wheeler, and Connor, who each have more than 250 goals.
17. A. Connor Hellebuyck. He also leads the organization with nearly 300 wins and more than 170 losses.
18. D. Paul Maurice. He won 315 games over nine seasons behind the bench, and Bob Hartley is second on the list with 136 wins.

Did You Know?

The 1998 Winter Olympics marked the first time the NHL participated in the games, pausing the season to allow their players to represent their countries.

CHAPTER 26:
THE PACIFIC DIVISION PART 1

1. Which Anaheim Ducks player leads the organization in games played and is the only player with more than 1,000 games in the Ducks sweater?

    A. Corey Perry
    B. Cam Fowler
    C. Teemu Selanne
    D. Ryan Getzlaf

2. Which Ducks player is only fourth on the team's all-time games played list but at the top of the all-time goals list for the organization?

    A. Corey Perry
    B. Paul Kariya
    C. Teemu Selanne
    D. Jakob Silfverberg

3. Though he may lose the top spot during the 2024–25 season, which Ducks goaltender leads the team in all-time wins?

    A. Guy Hebert
    B. Jean-Sebastien Giguere
    C. Jonas Hiller
    D. Frederik Andersen

4. Which coach was behind the Ducks' bench for ten seasons in total, with his final year coming in 2019? He leads the team in all-time wins.

    A. Bruce Boudreau
    B. Ron Wilson
    C. Mike Babcock
    D. Randy Carlyle

5. The Calgary Flames have played 52 NHL seasons, and which player holds the record for most games played?

    A. Jarome Iginla
    B. Mikael Backlund
    C. Mark Giordano
    D. Robyn Regehr

6. Which Calgary Flames player has the all-time most assists for the team, only 39 more than Jarome Iginla?

A. Theo Fleury
  B. Gary Suter
  C. Johnny Gaudreau
  D. Al MacInnis

7. Which tough Flames player leads the organization substantially in penalty minutes?

   A. Gary Roberts
   B. Tim Hunter
   C. Joel Otto
   D. Jim Peplinski

8. Which Flames goalie is the only one to surpass 300 wins with the team?

   A. Dan Bouchard
   B. Mike Vernon
   C. Miikka Kiprusoff
   D. Rejean Lemelin

9. The Calgary Flames have had 21 coaches in their history, but which one not only won the most games but also had the longest tenure?

   A. Darryl Sutter
   B. Bob Johnson
   C. Fred Creighton
   D. Terry Crisp

10. The Edmonton Oilers have a rich, storied history. Which player has the most games for the team, though?

    A. Ryan Smyth
    B. Ryan Nugent-Hopkins
    C. Kevin Lowe
    D. Mark Messier

11. Though he is not in the top ten of games played for the team, which player leads the Oilers in goals, assists, and points?

    A. Jari Kurri
    B. Glenn Anderson
    C. Mark Messier
    D. Wayne Gretzky

12. Which player has the all-time most penalty minutes for the Oilers?
    A. Kevin McClelland
    B. Kevin Lowe
    C. Mark Messier
    D. Kelly Buchberger

13. The Oilers only have one goaltender with more than 200 career wins with the team. Which player is it?
    A. Bill Ranford
    B. Tommy Salo
    C. Grant Fuhr
    D. Andy Moog

14. Which Oilers coach led the team through their dynasty of the 1980s and therefore easily leads the organization in the win column?
    A. Craig MacTavish
    B. Glen Sather
    C. Ron Low
    D. Todd McLellan

15. The Los Angeles Kings have participated in 57 NHL seasons. Which player has the most games for the team?
    A. Dustin Brown
    B. Anze Kopitar
    C. Drew Doughty
    D. Dave Taylor

16. Which Los Angeles Kings player leads the organization in goals, though only by a few?
    A. Luc Robitaille
    B. Marcel Dionne
    C. Dave Taylor
    D. Anze Kopitar

17. Which Los Angeles Kings goaltender has more than double the number of wins of any other goaltender on the list?
    A. Rogie Vachon
    B. Kelly Hrudey

    C. Mario Lessard
    D. Jonathan Quick

18. Which Los Angeles Kings player leads the organization in all-time penalty minutes?
    A. Rob Blake
    B. Jay Wells
    C. Marty McSorley
    D. Dave Taylor

Chapter 26 Answers:

1. D. Ryan Getzlaf. He played 1,157 games for the team and leads the club in all-time assists and points.
2. C. Teemu Selanne. He scored 457 goals in 966 games with the team, and he's well ahead of Corey Perry, who is in second place with 372 goals.
3. B. Jean-Sebastien Giguere. He has 206 wins during his time with the team, but John Gibson is closing the gap as the 2024–25 season gets underway.
4. D. Randy Carlyle. He won 384 games with the team during those seasons, with a win percentage of .587.
5. A. Jarome Iginla. Iginla played 1,219 games with the Flames organization and leads the team in all-time goals and points.
6. D. Al MacInnis. The stout defenseman had 609 assists for the team during his 803 games there, with Iginla in second place and Fleury, Suter, and Gaudreau rounding out the top five.
7. B. Tim Hunter. His 2,405 penalty minutes are almost 700 ahead of Gary Roberts, who had 1,736 penalty minutes during his career with the team.
8. C. Miikka Kiprusoff. He won 305 games to 192 losses, both of which lead the team. Mike Vernon is second on the list with 262 wins.
9. A. Darryl Sutter. He won 210 games during six seasons with the team. He's the only coach to last that long.
10. C. Kevin Lowe. He is the only player, as of 2024, with more than 1,000 games with the organization.
11. D. Wayne Gretzky. The Great One scored 583 goals and tallied 1,086 assists during his time with the Oilers organization. Connor McDavid recently passed Mark Messier for second place on the all-time assists list.
12. D. Kelly Buchberger. He collected 1,747 penalty minutes, and McClelland is in second place at 1,289 minutes.
13. C. Grant Fuhr. He has 226 wins in his career with the Oilers. Bill Ranford is second with 167 wins, but Ranford also leads the team with 193 losses.
14. B. Glen Sather. He won 464 games with the team from 1980 to 1994. It was a winning percentage of .616.

15. B. Anze Kopitar. He has played almost 1,400 games going into the 2024–25 season and leads the organization in all-time assists.
16. A. Luc Robitaille. He scored 557 goals for the team. Dionne scored 550, while Taylor and Kopitar have both scored over 400.
17. D. Jonathan Quick. Quick won 370 games with the Kings before moving on. The next closest goalie, Rogie Vachon, won 171 games with the team.
18. C. Marty McSorley. He collected 1,846 penalty minutes during his time with the team in his enforcer role.

Did You Know?

The Ottawa Senators won the first Stanley Cup ever awarded to the NHL Champions in 1927.

CHAPTER 27:
THE PACIFIC DIVISION PART 2

1. In 32 NHL seasons, the San Jose Sharks have made the playoffs how many times?

    A. 21
    B. 23
    C. 24
    D. 25

2. Which Sharks player spent more than 1,600 games with the team, more than any other player?

    A. Marc-Edouard Vlasic
    B. Joe Thornton
    C. Joe Pavelski
    D. Patrick Marleau

3. Which player leads the San Jose Sharks in all-time assists and is 200 assists ahead of second place?

    A. Joe Pavelski
    B. Brent Burns
    C. Joe Thornton
    D. Patrick Marleau

4. Only one San Jose Sharks goaltender has more than 200 wins, as of 2024. Which of these goaltenders has that accomplishment to his name?

    A. Martin Jones
    B. Evgeni Nabokov
    C. Antti Niemi
    D. Vesa Toskala

5. In the Sharks' 32 seasons, they have had 11 coaches, with a 12th coach beginning in 2024–25. Which of them has the most victories behind the bench?

    A. Ron Wilson
    B. Peter DeBoer
    C. Darryl Sutter
    D. Todd McLellan

6. The Seattle Kraken played in three seasons before the 2024–25 season. How many of those seasons resulted in a playoff appearance?

A. Zero
   B. One
   C. Two
   D. Three

7. Though the team is young, one Seattle Kraken player has already scored 100 goals for the team. Who is it?

   A. Jared McCann
   B. Jordan Eberle
   C. Yanni Gourde
   D. Matty Beniers

8. Though the Seattle Kraken have only had four goaltenders win a game for the team, which goalie reached 50 wins first?

   A. Philipp Grubauer
   B. Joey Daccord
   C. Martin Jones
   D. Chris Driedger

9. The Seattle Kraken have only had two coaches in their history. Who was the first one?

   A. Dan Bylsma
   B. Gerard Gallant
   C. Dave Hakstol
   D. John Tortorella

10. In 53 NHL seasons for the Vancouver Canucks, which player leads the team in all-time games played?

    A. Daniel Sedin
    B. Henrik Sedin
    C. Trevor Linden
    D. Alexander Edler

11. Which Canucks player leads the organization in goals but not in assists or points?

    A. Trevor Linden
    B. Markus Naslund
    C. Henrik Sedin
    D. Daniel Sedin

12. Only one Vancouver Canucks player has amassed more than 2,000 penalty minutes. Who is it?

    A. Garth Butcher
    B. Stan Smyl
    C. Gino Odjick
    D. Harold Snepsts

13. Two Canucks goalies have won more than 200 games with the team. Which one has the most (and a much better record than the other)?

    A. Roberto Luongo
    B. Kirk McLean
    C. Richard Brodeur
    D. Thatcher Demko

14. Behind the bench, two Canucks coaches have lasted for seven seasons, but one enjoyed much more success. Who has the most wins for the organization?

    A. Marc Crawford
    B. Alain Vigneault
    C. Harry Neale
    D. Pat Quinn

15. Going into the 2024–25 season, which Vegas Golden Knights player has a slight lead when it comes to total games played for the club?

    A. William Karlsson
    B. Jonathan Marchessault
    C. Shea Theodore
    D. Brayden McNabb

16. Three Golden Knights players have scored more than 100 goals with the team. Who has the most?

    A. Jonathan Marchessault
    B. William Karlsson
    C. Reilly Smith
    D. Max Pacioretty

17. Only one Vegas Golden Knights goaltender has notched more than 100 wins with the team. Who is it?
    A. Logan Thompson
    B. Adin Hill
    C. Marc-Andre Fleury
    D. Robin Lehner

18. Before the beginning of the 2024–25 season, Gerard Gallant had the most wins as a Vegas Golden Knights coach. How many games did he win in his almost three full seasons with the team?
    A. 105
    B. 109
    C. 118
    D. 124

Chapter 27 Answers:

1. A. 21. Though they have not yet won a Stanley Cup, their playoff appearances are bound to pay off eventually.
2. D. Patrick Marleau. He played 300 more games than Vlasic, who played almost 200 more games than Thornton.
3. C. Joe Thornton. Thornton collected 804 assists in his 1,104 games with the San Jose Sharks.
4. B. Evgeni Nabokov. He won 293 games for the team while only losing 178. Martin Jones is second on the list with 170.
5. D. Todd McLellan. He won 311 games in seven seasons with the team, leading the organization with a .637-win percentage.
6. B. One. They made the playoffs during the 2022–23 season, their second season in the league. They also defeated Colorado to advance to the second round of that playoff run.
7. A. Jared McCann. At one point during the 2024–25 season, he had a 40-goal lead on every other Seattle Kraken player for the all-time Kraken goal list.
8. A. Philipp Grubauer. The other three goaltenders all have more than ten wins with the franchise as well.
9. C. Dave Hakstol. He coached the team for their first three seasons, winning 107 games and losing 112.
10. B. Henrik Sedin. He played 1,330 games for the team, only 24 more than his brother, Daniel.
11. D. Daniel Sedin. He scored 393 goals for the Canucks, and he trails his brother Henrik by only 29 points on the all-time Canucks list.
12. C. Gino Odjick. He collected 2,127 penalty minutes with the Canucks, well ahead of Garth Butcher, who had 1,668 penalty minutes.
13. A. Roberto Luongo. He won 252 games with the team, and he lost 137. Kirk McLean won 211 games with the Canucks, but he also leads the team with 228 losses in goal.
14. B. Alain Vigneault. He won 313 games for the team over seven seasons, with a points percentage of .632. Crawford had 236 wins but only a .554-points percentage.
15. A. Brayden McNabb. He is slightly ahead of Karlsson and Marchessault with over 500 games played for the team.

16. A. Jonathan Marchessault. He has nearly 200 goals for the team, while Karlsson has a bit over 150.
17. C. Marc-Andre Fleury. He won 117 games with the team, including a whopping 23 shutouts. Thompson has a little over 50 wins and is in the single digits when it comes to shutouts.
18. C. 118. He had 75 losses, giving him a points percentage of .601, which is currently the worst of the three coaches in Vegas team history.

Did You Know?

Jacques Plante has his name on the Stanley Cup five times, but it is spelled differently each time!

CHAPTER 28:
MVP SEASONS

1. In 2011, which forward led the NHL in scoring on his way to the league MVP?

    A. Steven Stamkos
    B. Corey Perry
    C. Jarome Iginla
    D. Daniel Sedin

2. For the 2009–10 season, which player led the league with 112 points and narrowly beat Alex Ovechkin in MVP voting?

    A. Ilya Bryzgalov
    B. Ryan Miller
    C. Sidney Crosby
    D. Henrik Sedin

3. In 2003–04, which great player led the league in scoring and had an impressive +35 on the plus/minus rating?

    A. Markus Naslund
    B. Jarome Iginla
    C. Martin St. Louis
    D. Joe Sakic

4. Which player won the 2002–03 MVP with 106 points on the season and an incredible +52 on plus/minus? His linemate was also +52 but did not get any first-place votes.

    A. Peter Forsberg
    B. Markus Naslund
    C. Joe Thornton
    D. Todd Bertuzzi

5. Which goalie had a dominant season for his team in 2002–03, though he couldn't help to end the Canadian drought on the Stanley Cup?

    A. Dominik Hasek
    B. Patrick Roy
    C. Jose Theodore
    D. Nikolai Khabibulin

6. Which big defenseman dominated and played incredibly during the 1999–2000 season, posting a +52 plus/minus for his team?

- A. Chris Pronger
- B. Nicklas Lidstrom
- C. Adam Foote
- D. Rob Blake

7. Which goaltender had a great season in 1997–98, nearly dragging his team through the playoffs by himself?

   - A. Ed Belfour
   - B. Olaf Kolzig
   - C. Chris Osgood
   - D. Dominik Hasek

8. Which 26-year-old forward was the league's leading scorer by a lot during the 1998–99 season?

   - A. Alexei Yashin
   - B. Jaromir Jagr
   - C. Teemu Selanne
   - D. Eric Lindros

9. Which strong forward won the Hart Trophy during the 1994–95 season, two years before he would help his team reach the Stanley Cup Finals?

   - A. Joe Juneau
   - B. Steve Yzerman
   - C. Eric Lindros
   - D. Brett Hull

10. Which player was traded during the 2005–06 season, then went on to win the league MVP that season?

    - A. Jaromir Jagr
    - B. Eric Staal
    - C. Daniel Alfredsson
    - D. Joe Thornton

11. Which great player won the league MVP in 1990, even after his incredible teammate was traded away?

    - A. Mark Messier
    - B. Ray Bourque
    - C. Brett Hull

D. Wayne Gretzky

12. In the 2016-17 season, which player put up 100 points to lead the league in scoring and win the Hart?

    A. Sidney Crosby
    B. Connor McDavid
    C. Brent Burns
    D. Patrick Kane

13. In 2006-07, which young superstar showed that he was more than ready to lead his franchise into the future, and the Hart Trophy was proof?

    A. Vincent Lecavalier
    B. Scott Niedermayer
    C. Sidney Crosby
    D. Daniel Briere

14. In 1962-63, which 34-year-old player scored 86 points to lead the league, showing that he wasn't ready to give up his spot to the young guns?

    A. Stan Mikita
    B. Alex Delvecchio
    C. Frank Mahovlich
    D. Gordie Howe

15. In the 1968-69 season, which Boston Bruins player posted a gaudy 126 points to win the Hart?

    A. Bobby Orr
    B. Phil Esposito
    C. Ted Green
    D. Bobby Hull

16. In the 1970-71 season, which player did not lead the league in scoring, but his +124 was an incredible show of dominance?

    A. Phil Esposito
    B. Bobby Hull
    C. Bobby Orr
    D. Dave Keon

17. Which player did not win the Hart in 1989 but came within one point of being only the second player to score 200 points in one season?
    A. Mario Lemieux
    B. Wayne Gretzky
    C. Steve Yzerman
    D. Chris Chelios

18. Until Connor McDavid won unanimously in 2021, who was the only player to win the Hart Trophy unanimously, back in 1982?
    A. Brian Trottier
    B. Mike Bossy
    C. Wayne Gretzky
    D. Peter Stastny

Chapter 28 Answers:

1. B. Corey Perry. Perry scored 50 goals and added 48 assists for 98 points on the season. Sedin had 104 points but did not get the majority of votes for the trophy.
2. D. Henrik Sedin. He only scored 29 goals that season, but the 83 assists helped him to the scoring lead.
3. C. Martin St. Louis. The small forward scored 38 goals and 56 assists that season, and he was the only player in the league during that season to tally more than 90 points.
4. A. Peter Forsberg. Forsberg had 29 goals and 77 assists on the season. He earned 38 first-place votes, and Martin Brodeur had 14.
5. C. Jose Theodore. He posted a .931 save percentage, a 2.11 GAA, and seven shutouts for the Montreal Canadiens. Roy finished third in voting with a .925 save percentage and a 1.94 GAA.
6. A. Chris Pronger. His 62 points were not the most among defensemen, but when you're +50 on the season, it means you're dominating the ice!
7. D. Dominik Hasek. His .932 save percentage, 2.09 GAA, and 13 shutouts got Buffalo a sixth seed in the East, then they streaked to the Conference Finals before falling to Washington.
8. B. Jaromir Jagr. He had a total of 127 points on the season, 20 more than the next closest player, Selanne.
9. C. Eric Lindros. He scored 29 goals and added 41 assists for a 70-point season in 48 games.
10. D. Joe Thornton. He scored 125 points between Boston and San Jose on his way to the Hart Trophy.
11. A. Mark Messier. He scored 129 points and had a +19 with the Oilers, even after Gretzky had been traded to Los Angeles.
12. B. Connor McDavid. He was the only player that season to notch 100 points, and he was +27 with the Oilers.
13. C. Sidney Crosby. He posted 120 points, including 84 assists, to help a rebuilding Penguins team.
14. D. Gordie Howe. He was the oldest player to receive first-place votes; the other forwards with votes were in their early to mid-20s.
15. B. Phil Esposito. It was an impressive season, but he scored 152 points a couple of seasons later and did not win the Hart.

16. C. Bobby Orr. Orr scored 139 points as a defenseman to win the Hart Trophy. Esposito had 152 points, but Orr's dominating play could not be ignored.
17. A. Mario Lemieux. He had 114 assists and 85 goals, but the Hart Trophy still went to Gretzky, who posted 168 points that season.
18. C. Wayne Gretzky. He had 92 goals and 120 assists, for a whopping 212 points. He was also +80 on the season.

Did You Know?

A Gordie Howe hat trick is when a player gets a goal, an assist, and a penalty for fighting all in one game. Despite the name, Howe only had two of these in his playing career.

CHAPTER 29:
STANLEY CUP CHAMPIONSHIPS

1. The Carolina Hurricanes won their first Stanley Cup during what year, when they defeated the Edmonton Oilers?

    A. 2006
    B. 2007
    C. 2008
    D. 2010

2. In 1998, which team won their second Cup in two years, after one of their defensemen suffered a career-ending injury in a car accident the previous summer?

    A. Washington Capitals
    B. Philadelphia Flyers
    C. Detroit Red Wings
    D. Colorado Avalanche

3. In 1984, the New York Islanders' dynasty came to an end, and they passed the torch to which team?

    A. Montreal Canadiens
    B. Toronto Maple Leafs
    C. Boston Bruins
    D. Edmonton Oilers

4. In 1994, which Original Six team broke a 54-year streak to win the Stanley Cup?

    A. Boston Bruins
    B. New York Rangers
    C. Chicago Blackhawks
    D. Detroit Red Wings

5. Against the Mighty Ducks in 2003, which team stood tall to win their third Cup in nine seasons?

    A. Dallas Stars
    B. Philadelphia Flyers
    C. New Jersey Devils
    D. Buffalo Sabres

6. In 2010, which team defeated the Philadelphia Flyers to win their first Cup in 49 years?

    A. Detroit Red Wings
    B. Chicago Blackhawks

C. Toronto Maple Leafs
   D. San Jose Sharks

7. One year after Chicago's Cup drought came to an end, which team ended an almost 40-year drought?

   A. Boston Bruins
   B. St. Louis Blues
   C. Los Angeles Kings
   D. Vegas Golden Knights

8. In 1950, Pete Babando scored the Cup-winning goal in double overtime of Game 7 for which team?

   A. New York Rangers
   B. Montreal Canadiens
   C. Toronto Maple Leafs
   D. Detroit Red Wings

9. In 1980, which team began a dynasty when they defeated the Philadelphia Flyers to win the Cup?

   A. Edmonton Oilers
   B. New York Islanders
   C. Boston Bruins
   D. Montreal Canadiens

10. The Chicago Blackhawks beat which team in 2013 to win their second Cup in three years?

    A. Tampa Bay Lightning
    B. New York Rangers
    C. Boston Bruins
    D. New Jersey Devils

11. When this team won the Stanley Cup in 2014, it was their second Cup in three seasons. Which team was it?

    A. New York Rangers
    B. Dallas Stars
    C. Boston Bruins
    D. Los Angeles Kings

12. In 2015, the Chicago Blackhawks won the Cup again, beating which team in six games?

A. Florida Panthers
   B. Pittsburgh Penguins
   C. Tampa Bay Lightning
   D. Montreal Canadiens

13. The Pittsburgh Penguins defeated which team in 2016 to win the Stanley Cup?
   A. San Jose Sharks
   B. Los Angeles Kings
   C. Colorado Avalanche
   D. Arizona Coyotes

14. One year later, the Penguins won their second-straight Cup when they beat which team?
   A. Los Angeles Kings
   B. Vegas Golden Knights
   C. Dallas Stars
   D. Nashville Predators

15. In 2018, which team won their first Stanley Cup in team history?
   A. Vegas Golden Knights
   B. Washington Capitals
   C. St. Louis Blues
   D. Anaheim Ducks

16. One year after the Capitals won their first Cup, which other team won theirs?
   A. Vegas Golden Knights
   B. St. Louis Blues
   C. Anaheim Ducks
   D. Winnipeg Jets

17. Which team won the Stanley Cup in both 2020 and 2021?
   A. Colorado Avalanche
   B. Vegas Golden Knights
   C. Dallas Stars
   D. Tampa Bay Lightning

18. Which team lost the Stanley Cup Finals in 2023, only to come back and win it in 2024?

A. Edmonton Oilers
B. Vegas Golden Knights
C. Florida Panthers
D. St. Louis Blues

Chapter 29 Answers:

1. A. 2006. The Hurricanes needed all seven games to win, and goaltender Cam Ward took home Playoff MVP honors.
2. C. Detroit Red Wings. Vladimir Konstantinov was severely injured in the accident, but the team still rallied to win.
3. D. Edmonton Oilers. That season, Gretzky and Messier delivered Edmonton its first of many Stanley Cups.
4. B. New York Rangers. Mark Messier came from Edmonton to help the Big Apple win their first in a very long time.
5. C. New Jersey Devils. They needed seven games to overcome the Ducks, and Ducks goalie Jean-Sebastien Giguere was named MVP.
6. B. Chicago Blackhawks. Patrick Kane scored the Cup-winning goal in overtime of Game 6.
7. A. Boston Bruins. They defeated the Vancouver Canucks in seven games.
8. D. Detroit Red Wings. They defeated the New York Rangers, even without Gordie Howe.
9. B. New York Islanders. They won the series in six games, and Bryan Trottier was named MVP.
10. C. Boston Bruins. The Blackhawks won the series in six games, including a triple-overtime Game 1.
11. D. Los Angeles Kings. The Kings beat the Rangers in five games, with Alec Martinez scoring the Cup-winning goal in double overtime of Game 5.
12. C. Tampa Bay Lightning. The Blackhawks won in six games, and defenseman Duncan Keith was named Playoffs MVP. He also scored the series-winning goal.
13. A. San Jose Sharks. The Penguins needed six games to win the series, and Pittsburgh captain Sidney Crosby was named the Playoffs MVP.
14. D. Nashville Predators. It was the first time since 1998 that a team successfully defended their Stanley Cup title.
15. B. Washington Capitals. They defeated the Vegas Golden Knights in five games, and their longtime captain, Alexander Ovechkin, was named Playoffs MVP.

16. B. St. Louis Blues. The Blues defeated the Boston Bruins in seven games, including Game 7 on the road, to win the Cup. Ryan O'Reilly was named Playoffs MVP.
17. D. Tampa Bay Lightning. They beat the Montreal Canadiens and Colorado Avalanche to win their two most recent championships.
18. C. Florida Panthers. They lost to the Vegas Golden Knights, but they returned one year later to beat the Oilers in seven games.

Did You Know?

The Florida Panthers used to throw toy rats on the ice to celebrate goals, and the Detroit Red Wings' fans often throw raw octopus on the ice during the playoffs.

CHAPTER 30:
HOCKEY HALL OF FAME

1. Three NHL players returned to the league after being inducted into the Hockey Hall of Fame. Which of these players did not?

    A. Guy Lafleur
    B. Wayne Gretzky
    C. Gordie Howe
    D. Mario Lemieux

2. In special circumstances, the induction period was waived for special players. How many players had the induction period waived?

    A. Seven
    B. Eight
    C. Nine
    D. Ten

3. Angela James and which other woman were the first women players inducted into the Hockey Hall of Fame in 2010?

    A. Geraldine Heaney
    B. Angela Ruggiero
    C. Cammi Granato
    D. Danielle Goyette

4. In 1968, only one player was inducted into the Hall of Fame. Who was it?

    A. Turk Broda
    B. Neil Colville
    C. Harry Oliver
    D. Bill Cowley

5. Three defensemen were inducted into the Hockey Hall of Fame in 2004. Which of these defensemen were not inducted that year?

    A. Ray Bourque
    B. Paul Coffey
    C. Larry Murphy
    D. Viacheslav Fetisov

6. Only two people were inducted into the Hockey Hall of Fame in 2006. One was Dick Duff, and the other was which legendary goaltender?

A. Grant Fuhr
   B. Patrick Roy
   C. Ed Belfour
   D. Billy Smith

7. In 2009, four players were inducted into the Hockey Hall of Fame. Which of them was not a member of the 2001–02 Detroit Red Wings?

   A. Steve Yzerman
   B. Brett Hull
   C. Brian Leetch
   D. Luc Robitaille

8. In 2011, two Canadian centers were inducted into the Hockey Hall of Fame. One was Joe Nieuwendyk. The other played for seven different NHL teams during his 20-year NHL career. Who was it?

   A. Adam Oates
   B. Joe Sakic
   C. Doug Gilmour
   D. Steve Yzerman

9. Four players were inducted in 2012. Three were centers, but which one was the right wing?

   A. Pavel Bure
   B. Adam Oates
   C. Joe Sakic
   D. Mats Sundin

10. Rob Blake, Peter Forsberg, Dominik Hasek, and Mike Modano were inducted in 2014. As players, how many Stanley Cups did they win altogether?

    A. Four
    B. Five
    C. Six
    D. Seven

11. In 2015, four defensemen and one center were inducted into the Hall of Fame. The center also played some defense during his career. Who was it?

A. Eric Lindros
   B. Henrik Sedin
   C. Guy Carbonneau
   D. Sergei Fedorov

12. In 2017, a group of four wingers were inducted into the Hall of Fame, but only one hailed from Europe. Who was it?

    A. Dave Andreychuk
    B. Paul Kariya
    C. Mark Recchi
    D. Teemu Selanne

13. Which goaltender reached the Hall of Fame in 2018 and still holds many NHL records to this day?

    A. Patrick Roy
    B. Martin Brodeur
    C. Dominik Hasek
    D. Henrik Lundqvist

14. Guy Carbonneau and which teammate of his were inducted into the Hockey Hall of Fame in 2019?

    A. Mark Recchi
    B. Mike Modano
    C. Sergei Zubov
    D. Joe Nieuwendyk

15. In 2020, Marian Hossa was inducted into the Hockey Hall of Fame. How many goals did he score in 1,309 NHL games?

    A. 470
    B. 525
    C. 560
    D. 593

16. Which right wing was inducted in 2022, and although he did not win a Stanley Cup, he did win a gold medal with Sweden in 2006?

    A. Daniel Alfredsson
    B. Jarome Iginla
    C. Nicklas Lidstrom
    D. Peter Forsberg

17. In 2023, three goaltenders were inducted into the Hall of Fame. Which of these was not one of them?

   A. Tom Barrasso
   B. Roberto Luongo
   C. Mike Vernon
   D. Henrik Lundqvist

18. In 2024, which Russian center was inducted into the Hall of Fame?

   A. Igor Larionov
   B. Sergei Fedorov
   C. Sergei Makarov
   D. Pavel Datsyuk

Chapter 30 Answers:

1. B. Wayne Gretzky. The Great One did not return to the league, while the other three players did. Mario Lemieux did so most recently when he returned in 2000.
2. D. Ten. Most recently, Wayne Gretzky was given such an honor in 1999, right after he retired from the league. Now, the Selection Committee cannot give that honor anymore.
3. C. Cammi Granato. As of 2024, 12 women players have been inducted into the Hall.
4. D. Bill Cowley. He played 13 seasons for the St. Louis Eagles and the Boston Bruins as a center.
5. D. Viacheslav Fetisov. He was inducted in 2001, while the other three choices were inducted in 2004 as the only three selections that year.
6. B. Patrick Roy. He won four Stanley Cups as a player, along with three Conn Smythe Trophies and three Vezina Trophies.
7. C. Brian Leetch. Leetch won one Stanley Cup with the New York Rangers in 1994, along with two Norris Trophies.
8. C. Doug Gilmour. He played for the Blues, Flames, Maple Leafs, Devils, Blackhawks, Sabres, and Canadiens.
9. A. Pavel Bure. He played right wing and spent his career with the Canucks, Panthers, and Rangers.
10. C. Six. Modano had one, Hasek two, Blake one, and Forsberg two.
11. D. Sergei Fedorov. Fedorov's NHL career was spent with the Red Wings, Ducks, Blue Jackets, and Capitals. He won three Stanley Cups with Detroit.
12. D. Teemu Selanne. He won one Stanley Cup in 2007 with the Ducks. He was also named to the Jets Hall of Fame in 2022.
13. B. Martin Brodeur. He leads the NHL in all-time regular season wins, losses, and shutouts, among other records.
14. C. Sergei Zubov. Zubov spent most of his NHL career with the Dallas Stars. He won one Cup with them and another with the 1994 New York Rangers.
15. B. 525. Hossa famously played in three straight Stanley Cup Finals for three different teams. He only won on his third try. In the end, all three of his Stanley Cups were with the Blackhawks.

16. A. Daniel Alfredsson. Alfredsson had 444 goals in 1,246 games with Ottawa and Detroit.
17. B. Roberto Luongo. He was inducted in 2022, and though he never won a Stanley Cup as a player, he did win one as an executive with the Florida Panthers in 2024.
18. D. Pavel Datsyuk. Datsyuk won two Stanley Cups with the Detroit Red Wings in 2002 and 2008.

Did You Know?

Fifteen different goaltenders have scored goals in the NHL. Martin Brodeur has three.

CHAPTER 31:
UNBEATABLE RECORDS

1. Wayne Gretzky has long held the NHL record for career points with how many?

    A. 2,587
    B. 2,785
    C. 2,857
    D. 2,875

2. Wayne Gretzky also holds the record for most goals in a single season. How many goals did he score during that record-breaking 1981–82 season?

    A. 92
    B. 87
    C. 86
    D. 85

3. The Great One also holds the record for most points in one season. How many of the top five spots does he hold?

    A. Two
    B. Three
    C. Four
    D. Five

4. Darryl Sittler holds the NHL record for most points in a single game. How many did he get?

    A. Seven
    B. Eight
    C. Nine
    D. Ten

5. Going into the 2024–25 season, Alexander Ovechkin can catch Wayne Gretzky's career goal record. How many career goals did Gretzky score?

    A. 844
    B. 894
    C. 874
    D. 849

6. Wayne Gretzky's dominant career earned him many Art Ross Trophies as the league's top scorer. How many did he win in a row?

A. Five
B. Six
C. Seven
D. Eight

7. Which NHL player holds the record for most goals scored by a rookie, with 76 goals?

    A. Mike Bossy
    B. Teemu Selanne
    C. Alex Ovechkin
    D. Joe Nieuwendyk

8. Which NHL player holds the record for most games played, which he earned over 23 seasons in the league?

    A. Patrick Marleau
    B. Gordie Howe
    C. Mark Messier
    D. Jaromir Jagr

9. Which goaltender has the most all-time wins and is the only one to have more than 600 wins?

    A. Roberto Luongo
    B. Patrick Roy
    C. Marc-Andre Fleury
    D. Martin Brodeur

10. Martin Brodeur owns the record for most career shutouts, but who did he pass at the top of the list?

    A. Glenn Hall
    B. George Hainsworth
    C. Terry Sawchuk
    D. Jacques Plante

11. Because the game is played differently today, which player's record of most career penalty minutes likely won't be broken soon, if ever?

    A. Dale Hunter
    B. Dave Williams
    C. Tie Domi
    D. Marty McSorley

12. Alex Ovechkin passed which player at the top of the all-time power-play goals list?

    A. Brett Hull
    B. Luc Robitaille
    C. Teemu Selanne
    D. Dave Andreychuk

13. Wayne Gretzky is at the top of the career shorthanded goals list, but how many did he score?

    A. 73
    B. 63
    C. 53
    D. 43

14. As of 2024, which player holds the NHL record for most game-winning goals in a career?

    A. Alex Ovechkin
    B. Gordie Howe
    C. Jaromir Jagr
    D. Phil Esposito

15. Wayne Gretzky might lose his goal record, but he's going to keep his hat trick record for a very long time. How many did he have?

    A. 44
    B. 46
    C. 48
    D. 50

16. Which NHL player played every game from November 3, 2009 to April 13, 2023?

    A. Phil Kessel
    B. Keith Yandle
    C. Doug Jarvis
    D. Garry Unger

17. Which team made the playoffs 29 years in a row, beginning in 1967–68?

    A. Detroit Red Wings
    B. Boston Bruins

C. Chicago Blackhawks
   D. St. Louis Blues
18. Which goaltender holds the record for most wins in a single playoff run, with 18?
   A. Grant Fuhr
   B. Andrei Vasilevskiy
   C. Patrick Roy
   D. Martin Brodeur

Chapter 31 Answers:

1. C. 2,857. Gretzky's record includes a whopping 1,963 assists, another mark that will likely stand forever.
2. A. 92. He also holds second place with 87, while Brett Hull and Mario Lemieux had seasons of 86 and 85, respectively.
3. C. Four. He holds the top four spots with seasons of 215, 212, 208, and 205 points before Mario Lemieux breaks the streak with a season of 199 points.
4. D. Ten. He scored six goals and collected four assists for the Toronto Maple Leafs against the Boston Bruins on February 7, 1976.
5. B. 894. Ovechkin starts the 2024–25 season just 41 goals behind the record.
6. C. Seven. He won every one of them between 1981 and 1987. Mario Lemieux broke his streak in 1988.
7. B. Teemu Selanne. Selanne's 76 goals in 1992–93 are well ahead of Mike Bossy, who scored 53 goals in 73 games during the 1977–78 season.
8. A. Patrick Marleau. He played in 1,779 games with the Sharks, Maple Leafs, and Penguins, just 12 more games than Gordie Howe.
9. D. Martin Brodeur. His 691 wins puts him more than 100 ahead of the next closest goaltender, Marc-Andre Fleury.
10. C. Terry Sawchuk. Brodeur has the record with 125, and Sawchuk has 103, the only other goalie with more than 100.
11. B. Dave Williams. Dave "Tiger" Williams holds the record with 3,971 penalty minutes in 962 NHL games. Hunter, Domi, McSorley, and Bob Probert round out the top five.
12. D. Dave Andreychuk. Ovechkin has more than 300 power-play goals, at the top of the list after passing Andreychuk and his 274.
13. A. 73. He has ten more than Mark Messier, and Steve Yzerman has 50. Brad Marchand has less than 40.
14. C. Jaromir Jagr. He has 135 winners, though Ovechkin is likely to pass him during the 2024–25 season.
15. D. 50. Ovechkin has 31, so he is unlikely to catch Gretzky in that category.

16. A. Phil Kessel. His streak of 1,064 games will be a tough one to break. Brent Burns has an active streak of over 850, as of 2024.
17. B. Boston Bruins. Their streak came to an end when they missed the 1997 playoffs.
18. B. Andrei Vasilevskiy. It's not a typo. The 2020 playoffs had an extra round that was best of three. Unless the playoff rules are adjusted, this record will never be broken.

Did You Know?

The Stanley Cup weighs 34.5 pounds, so it's a bit of a chore to raise it over your head!

CHAPTER 32:
THE BIGGEST MOMENTS

1. Which defenseman is known for his "Flying Goal," which won his team the Stanley Cup in 1970?

    A. Brad Park
    B. Bobby Orr
    C. Denis Potvin
    D. Guy Lapointe

2. In 1981, Wayne Gretzky showed his scoring power when he scored his 50th goal of the season during which game?

    A. Game 39
    B. Game 42
    C. Game 45
    D. Game 47

3. Which player returned from cancer treatments in March 1993 to a standing ovation from the opposing team's fans?

    A. Pat LaFontaine
    B. Adam Oates
    C. Mario Lemieux
    D. Steve Yzerman

4. In March 1936, the longest playoff game in NHL history took place between Detroit and the Montreal Maroons. How many minutes did the game last?

    A. 168 minutes
    B. 171 minutes
    C. 174 minutes
    D. 176 minutes

5. In 1963, which player scored his 627th career goal, including playoffs, to become the all-time leading scorer?

    A. Maurice Richard
    B. Gordie Howe
    C. Wayne Gretzky
    D. Sid Abel

6. In 1994, which player guaranteed that his team would win the Stanley Cup—and then delivered?

    A. Wayne Gretzky
    B. Mario Lemieux

C. Mark Messier
   D. Scott Stevens

7. Which player scored the game-winning goal in Game 6 of the 1964 Stanley Cup Finals on a broken leg?

   A. Bobby Orr
   B. Bobby Baun
   C. Gordie Howe
   D. Alex Delvecchio

8. In March 2009, Martin Brodeur became the winningest goaltender of all time when his New Jersey Devils beat which team?

   A. Chicago Blackhawks
   B. Detroit Red Wings
   C. Boston Bruins
   D. New York Rangers

9. In 1952, Bill Mosienko scored the fastest hat trick in NHL history. How long did it take?

   A. One minute and 11 seconds
   B. 48 seconds
   C. 34 seconds
   D. 21 seconds

10. Which player returned from cancer treatment in 2002 and received a nine-minute standing ovation from the crowd?

    A. Brendan Morrison
    B. Ray Whitney
    C. Saku Koivu
    D. Andrew Cassels

11. The Toronto Maple Leafs rallied from being down 3–0 in the Stanley Cup Finals to win against which team in 1942?

    A. Boston Bruins
    B. Detroit Red Wings
    C. Montreal Canadiens
    D. New York Rangers

12. In the 1980 Winter Olympics, the United States beat which team to complete the "Miracle on Ice"?

- A. Sweden
- B. Finland
- C. Canada
- D. Soviet Union

13. Game 7 of the 1987 Patrick Division semifinals between the Islanders and Capitals is called the Easter Epic because it lasted how many overtime periods?
    - A. Two
    - B. Three
    - C. Four
    - D. Five

14. The Los Angeles Kings won their first Stanley Cup after beating the New York Rangers in how many games?
    - A. Four
    - B. Five
    - C. Six
    - D. Seven

15. In the 2024 Stanley Cup Finals, which team won their first Stanley Cup over the Edmonton Oilers with a win in Game 7?
    - A. Vegas Golden Knights
    - B. Seattle Kraken
    - C. Florida Panthers
    - D. Winnipeg Jets

16. Which Colorado Avalanche player was named Playoffs MVP after his team won the Stanley Cup in 2022?
    - A. Nathan MacKinnon
    - B. Gabriel Landeskog
    - C. Cale Makar
    - D. Mikko Rantanen

17. The 2019 St. Louis Blues needed seven games to defeat which team in the Stanley Cup Finals?
    - A. Philadelphia Flyers
    - B. New York Rangers
    - C. New York Islanders
    - D. Boston Bruins

18. The Pittsburgh Penguins won the 2009 Stanley Cup when Marc-Andre Fleury made a last-second save on which Red Wings player?
    A. Pavel Datsyuk
    B. Henrik Zetterberg
    C. Nicklas Lidstrom
    D. Brian Rafalski

Chapter 32 Answers:

1. B. Bobby Orr. The image of Orr flying through the air after scoring and being tripped has become one of the most recognizable images in hockey history.
2. A. Game 39. It had been a big deal for players to score 50 in 50, but Gretzky showed he didn't even need 40.
3. C. Mario Lemieux. Not only did he return after missing more than a dozen games but he still won the scoring title that season.
4. D. 176 minutes. The Red Wings' Mud Bruneteau scored the game-winning goal in that game.
5. B. Gordie Howe. He would hold the scoring record until Wayne Gretzky came onto the scene.
6. C. Mark Messier. He told the New York media that the Rangers would win, then he and his teammates made it happen.
7. B. Bobby Baun. His Maple Leafs went on to win Game 7 to take the Stanley Cup.
8. A. Chicago Blackhawks. It was Brodeur's 552nd win, but his career would end with 691 wins.
9. D. 21 seconds. He scored them against the New York Rangers, helping the Black Hawks come back from a four-goal deficit to win.
10. C. Saku Koivu. He finished his career with 255 goals and 577 assists in 1,124 games.
11. B. Detroit Red Wings. It is the only reverse sweep in the history of the Stanley Cup Finals.
12. D. Soviet Union. The US team was not expected to win the tournament, but they upset the Soviets.
13. C. Four. The Islanders won thanks to a goal from Pat LaFontaine.
14. B. Five. The final game included a double-overtime winner from Alec Martinez.
15. C. Florida Panthers. Connor McDavid of the Oilers was still named the MVP of the playoffs despite his team losing.
16. C. Cale Makar. The defenseman had 29 points in 20 games for the team, pushing them to victory.
17. D. Boston Bruins. Alex Pietrangelo scored the game-winning goal in that final Game 7, near the end of the first period.

18. C. Nicklas Lidstrom. Evgeni Malkin was named the MVP of the playoffs after the victory.

Did You Know?

Brett Hull's Cup-winning goal in 1999 remains a subject of controversy. His skate entered the crease, which some argue should have negated the goal.

CHAPTER 33:
THE ALL-STAR GAME

1. Which player went viral online, as fans voted him into the 2016 All-Star Game and helped him win MVP honors at that game?

    A. John Scott
    B. Patrick Kane
    C. Dylan Larkin
    D. Erik Karlsson

2. Several NHL players are tied for the most goals scored in a single All-Star Game. How many goals is the current mark?

    A. Three
    B. Four
    C. Five
    D. Six

3. The oldest player to play in an All-Star Game was Gordie Howe. How old was he when he played in the 1980 All-Star Game?

    A. 48
    B. 51
    C. 52
    D. 55

4. Which player holds the record for the fastest goal to start an All-Star Game?

    A. Ilya Kovalchuk
    B. Jarome Iginla
    C. Rick Nash
    D. Vincent Lecavalier

5. Which player remains the youngest to ever play in an All-Star Game?

    A. Steve Yzerman
    B. Alex Ovechkin
    C. Sidney Crosby
    D. Jeff Skinner

6. Which goaltender is the only one to win four straight All-Star Games?

    A. Patrick Roy
    B. Tim Thomas

C. Glenn Hall
   D. Dominik Hasek

7. Which player is the only one to ever score eight points in a single All-Star Game?

   A. Wayne Gretzky
   B. Mario Lemieux
   C. Sidney Crosby
   D. Sergei Fedorov

8. Joe Sakic played in 12 All-Star Games, collecting how many assists, more than any other player?

   A. 15
   B. 16
   C. 17
   D. 18

9. Which player collected four assists in one period during the 1993 All-Star Game?

   A. Adam Oates
   B. Pierre Turgeon
   C. Mark Recchi
   D. Ray Bourque

10. Which player scored the fastest two goals during the 1997 All-Star Game?

    A. Wayne Gretzky
    B. Brett Hull
    C. Paul Kariya
    D. Owen Nolan

11. The most assists in one game is five. Which of these players has not accomplished this mark?

    A. Mats Naslund
    B. Roman Josi
    C. Adam Oates
    D. Ryan O'Reilly

12. Which goaltender is the only one to have appearances in 13 All-Star Games?

A. Patrick Roy
B. Glenn Hall
C. Mike Vernon
D. Terry Sawchuk

13. Which All-Star team was the only team to be shut out in NHL history?

    A. 1967 NHL All-Stars
    B. 1992 Western Conference All-Stars
    C. 1996 Eastern Conference All-Stars
    D. 2002 World All-Stars

14. Which All-Star was a perfect four-for-four two years in a row in the Accuracy Shooting of the Skills Competition?

    A. Peter Forsberg
    B. Brendan Shanahan
    C. Mark Messier
    D. Ray Bourque

15. When the Breakaway Challenge was introduced in 2008, which player won it three years in a row?

    A. Patrick Kane
    B. Alexander Ovechkin
    C. Alex Pietrangelo
    D. Sidney Crosby

16. Of all the fastest skater times that have won the competition, which player was the slowest, winning the competition in 1999?

    A. Sami Kapanen
    B. Scott Niedermayer
    C. Peter Bondra
    D. Mike Gartner

17. The fastest shot during the NHL's Hardest Shot competition belongs to which player, as of 2024?

    A. Shea Weber
    B. Zdeno Chara
    C. Al Iafrate
    D. Victor Hedman

18. What is the All-Star Game record for the number of goals in one period by both teams?

    A. Seven
    B. Nine
    C. 11
    D. 13

Chapter 33 Answers:

1. A. John Scott. The enforcer was not known for his skills, but he helped put on a show and entertain the fans for that weekend.
2. B. Four. Wayne Gretzky set the record in 1983, and it was most recently tied by three players in 2019.
3. B. 51. Howe was very much celebrated as one of hockey's greatest players, even at his advanced age.
4. C. Rick Nash. He scored 12 seconds into the 2008 All-Star Game.
5. D. Jeff Skinner. He was 18 years and eight months old when he played in the 2011 All-Star Game.
6. B. Tim Thomas. He won every All-Star Game in which he played.
7. C. Sidney Crosby. He had four goals and four assists in the 2019 All-Star Game with the Metropolitan Division.
8. B. 16. Sakic collected the most, but he doesn't hold the record for most assists in one game.
9. A. Adam Oates. He helped Mike Gartner score a first-period hat trick with the assists as his team cruised to a 16–6 victory.
10. D. Owen Nolan. He scored twice in eight seconds for the Western Conference All-Stars.
11. C. Adam Oates. The other three players accomplished the number in 1988 (Naslund) and 2019 (Josi and O'Reilly).
12. B. Glenn Hall. He played a total of 540 minutes, which is another NHL record.
13. A. 1967 NHL All-Stars. They lost to the Montreal Canadiens by a score of 3–0.
14. D. Ray Bourque. He accomplished the feat in 1992 and 1993 to win that competition both times.
15. B. Alexander Ovechkin. Kane, Crosby, and Pietrangelo also won the competition once each.
16. C. Peter Bondra. His 1999 time was 14.640 seconds. He also won in 1997 with a 13.610.
17. B. Zdeno Chara. His shot of 108.8 mph is the fastest recorded during the competition. Martin Frk hit a 109.2 during the AHL All-Star competition in 2020.
18. C. 11. It took place in the second period of the 2015 All-Star Game.

Did You Know?

Helmets became mandatory in 1979 for NHL players, but older players in the league could choose to not wear one until their retirement.

CHAPTER 34:
HOCKEY'S ADVANCED STATISTICS

Can you identify some of these hockey statistics by their acronyms?

1. ATOI. Usually, defensemen lead in this category.
2. SV%. Goaltenders want this number to be high!
3. GAA. It's not a baby noise; it's another number to track a goalie's success.
4. SO. It's a good number for goalies and for the team's overall defense.
5. BLK. It can be painful, but it helps the team's defense.
6. FO%. It's an important metric for one of the key moments of any hockey game.
7. SH%. What are the chances it goes in?
8. SOG. It's not about soggy socks but getting pucks to where they need to go.
9. GWG. It's about scoring when it counts!
10. CF. An advanced stat involving shot attempts.
11. xG. How often is this going to happen? Depends on the quality.
12. ZS. It's all about having a good breakout.
13. GAR. But if this player's not playing, what's the difference?
14. WAR. If this player's gone, what's their record?
15. P/60. You can't play that much, but if you did, what would happen?
16. HDSV%. There's a difference between a one-timer and a dump-in.
17. OiSH%. What happens when this player is on the ice?
18. GSAA. Goalies like this number to be positive!

Chapter 34 Answers:

1. Average Time on Ice. This stat helps teams keep track of player usage and their workload.
2. Save Percentage. Goaltenders are often expected to have save percentages around .900 or .910.
3. Goals Against Average. This is how many goals a goalie allows per game. It's not always their fault, though!
4. Shutouts. When you don't allow a goal for an entire game, it's a team effort, but the goalie gets most of the credit.
5. Blocked Shots. When a player stops a shot from getting to their goaltender, it's a sign of a team playing good defense.
6. Faceoff Percentage. A center who wins a majority of their faceoffs is of great value to their team.
7. Shooting Percentage. A player who has a high shooting percentage takes quality shots and is more likely to score.
8. Shots on Goal. Teams who shoot more often score more.
9. Game-Winning Goals. A player who scores to give their team the lead gets a game-winning goal.
10. Corsi For. It measures shot attempts for a team while a specific player is on the ice.
11. Expected Goals. It measures how likely a shot attempt will become a goal.
12. Zone Starts. This stat measures where a player's shift starts, or where they most often take faceoffs.
13. Goals Above Replacement. It measures if a team scores more or less with a replacement instead of the player.
14. Wins Above Replacement. It measures if a team's record is better with or without a player.
15. Points Per 60 Minutes. If a player played 60 minutes, they would score this many points.
16. High-Danger Save Percentage. The goalie needs to save those quality scoring chances.
17. On-ice Save Percentage. Does a player help their goalie make more saves by reducing the quality of chances?
18. Goals Saved Above Average. It measures how many goals a goalie saves above the average of the rest of the league.

Did You Know?

The Detroit Red Wings' Steve Yzerman holds the NHL record for longest-serving captain, at 19 seasons over 20 years. One year was lost to a lockout.

CONCLUSION

There you have it! Thirty-four challenging chapters of hockey trivia, spanning the entire history of ice hockey and every single team in the NHL. There were plenty of names and facts in this book, so if you need to know more, you know exactly where to look!

Thanks to the internet, you can watch many of these moments and games whenever you want. You can see for yourself how goalies used to play without masks or how hockey players could get away with a lot more grabbing and hooking than they do today.

The chapters in this book also covered the early days of hockey and the leagues of that time. Plenty of players and teams made a big impact on the game, and those names deserve to be remembered!

And finally, if this book was too challenging, just try to go back through it again! You'll shock your friends and family with how much hockey knowledge you know just from these questions. Quiz those around you and help them learn about this amazing sport! And don't forget about those "Did You Know" facts at the end of each chapter. They give plenty of little tidbits that can be explored more!

Thank you for spending time with this book and the facts in these pages. Hockey is an amazing sport, and it should be spread far and wide to new fans and players. So, if you have all of these facts and stats memorized, saucer pass this book to a friend and let them experience the knowledge inside!

www.ingramcontent.com/pod-product-compliance
Lightning Source LLC
Chambersburg PA
CBHW060456030426
42337CB00015B/1610